AVAILABLE

A Memoir of
Heartbreak, Hookups,
Love, and Brunch

MATTESON PERRY

SCRIBNER
New York London Toronto Sydney New Delhi

For my wife,
who somehow managed to be
nothing but supportive of a book about
all the women I slept with before I met her

AVAILABLE

PROLOGUE

I Dated a Manic Pixie Dream Girl

ACT I

We lay next to each other in bed, sweaty and breathing hard. My air conditioner was doing its best to chase away the heat, but the New York City humidity hung in the air. Moonlight from the window illuminated the tattoo of a phoenix covering the left side of her torso. I traced it with my finger, from below her armpit, over the speed bumps of her ribs, to her hip bone. I had only seen tattoos like this in the movies, never in person, never this close, never in my own bed.

I had found my very own Manic Pixie Dream Girl.

The Manic Pixie Dream Girl has become the ingénue of millennials. Nathan Rabin coined the term while writing for *The A.V. Club* to describe the love interest in Cameron Crowe's *Elizabethtown*, but the character type has existed through the ages. Think Natalie Portman in *Garden State* or Audrey Hepburn in *Breakfast at Tiffany's*. Go back further and find Esmeralda from Victor Hugo's *The Hunchback of Notre-Dame*. Admittedly, she had mixed results in snapping Quasimodo out of the doldrums of life, but still, she qualifies.

The Manic Pixie Dream Girl, more a collection of quirks than a person, is the perfect love interest for the sensitive male protagonist. These weird (but always beautiful) girls appreciate shy, sad, creative boys and teach them to enjoy life again through sex, love, and various activities done in the rain.

Though often perky, the Manic Pixie Dream Girl is frequently troubled. She straddles the narrow line between quirky and crazy, mysterious and strange, sexy and slutty; she is perfectly imperfect. And imperfection is the key. A Manic Pixie Dream Girl must be messed up enough to need saving, so the powerless guy has something heroic to do in the third act.

I met my Manic Pixie Dream Girl, Kelly, in a sketch comedy class where, on the first day, she wore a bright red dress and cowboy boots. She had a look a guy might describe as "exotic," though she'd punch him in the arm if he used that term. She had a boyfriend, so we couldn't date, but we began chatting online, learning about each other's lives while trading YouTube clips of *Saturday Night Live* sketches.

One hot summer afternoon, we met at a bar with the intention of writing sketches together, but our plans changed, as they often do with Manic Pixie Dream Girls. We never opened our notebooks and instead went on an impromptu bar crawl. Each stop found us a bit drunker and soon our knees were touching under tables and our shoulders brushing together as we walked. The night ended with a drunken attempted kiss, by me, which she ducked.

"I can't cheat on my boyfriend," she said. "Even if things aren't going well and he doesn't understand me."

Not going well. There was hope. And I understood her. I understood her *so bad.*

We hugged goodbye and our skin, sticky from a day of sweating, stuck together slightly as we separated, a physical attestation of what I hoped we both felt. Turned out I was right. Within a month she broke up with her boyfriend, and not long after, she and her tattoo ended up in my bed.

ACT II

I'm not a socially awkward nerd by any means, but I'm not cool in the classic sense, either. For example, I secretly enjoy doing my taxes. Kelly, though, she was cool. She could instantly procure a drink at a hopelessly crowded bar and talk her way into invite-only parties. Being cool seemed so effortless for her and being around her made me feel cool by proxy. She was my human VIP pass.

My Manic Pixie Dream Girl was either all in or all out on everything she did, so things moved quickly. We spent that summer acting out our own "They're falling in love" movie montage. We lay in Central Park and stared at the sky; ate *moules-frites* at a dimly lit Brooklyn restaurant; tasted the salt on each other's skin after a night spent dancing; listened to the rain from bed (unfortunately there are no barns filled with straw in New York City, or we could have gone full Nicholas Sparks).

But it wasn't a blind "everything's perfect" love. Things about Kelly bothered me. I much preferred the Kelly I got when we were alone to the one who emerged at parties and bounced from person to person like a coked-up politician trying too hard to impress. She had a propensity for being late, suffered panic attacks, and had a streak of jealousy. She was my opposite in so many ways—impulsive, erratic, electric. But I loved Kelly anyway and this, for me, was a sign I'd found "true love." Kelly wasn't perfect, but she was perfectly imperfect. Within a year we moved to Los Angeles together.

ACT III

"What will happen to them if we break up?" Kelly asked. We were in a CB2 store, home of modern furniture that looks better in the showroom than in your house, discussing dining room chairs, our first big purchase as a couple.

I laughed off her question.

"I'm serious," she said.

"We're not going to break up," I said with a hug, "and if we do, what happens to these chairs will be the least of our worries."

Kelly wasn't convinced. On the ride home she played with her iPhone case, taking it on and off, on and off, as she stared out the window. We'd barely carried the chairs inside when the tears started. She paced around our mostly empty new apartment listing the reasons our relationship was doomed, why we shouldn't be buying things together.

The fight lasted several hours. Kelly attacked the soundness of our relationship while I defended it. My arguments were rational, while hers were rooted in emotion. Eventually, I logic-bullied her into surrender, convincing her that her emotions were wrong. Of course, a person's emotions can never be "wrong," even if they can't "defend" them, but for the moment I'd "won."

"I'm sorry about last night," she said the next morning. "I love the chairs and I love you."

"It's okay. I love you too," I said, before following up with the rallying cry of the Manic Pixie Dream Girl's boyfriend—"Everything's going to be all right."

Her smile said she believed me. It felt like I was "rescuing" her, and she seemed to like being "rescued."

As per the script, my Manic Pixie Dream Girl saved me from being a square in Act I, bringing excitement and coolness to my life, but here in Act III, it was my turn to do the saving. Being strong for her made me feel stronger. This feeling, of "fixing" someone, is the true gift of the Manic Pixie Dream Girl.

This is the moment when the movie usually ends, right after the man has told the Manic Pixie Dream Girl *everything will be all right* and fixed her with his love. Then the credits roll, pausing the story in a moment of eternal joy.

What makes movies magical is not that incredible things happen in them; incredible things happen in real life too. No, what makes movies magical is they end right after the incredible thing happens. They stop when the war is over, after the team wins the championship, after the boy gets the girl. But life keeps going, even when it's inconvenient for the narrative.

ACT IV
(The Act You Don't See in Movies)

Our relationship carried on for another two years and it was, for the most part, happy. I got along with her family. We had good sex. I made strides toward my goal of being a professional writer and Kelly had exciting things happening in her career. We got a dog too, at Kelly's prompting.

While jointly owning a dining room set terrified her, the idea of raising a living creature together didn't seem to faze her. We named the adorable beagle puppy Murray (after Bill Murray), and I felt like the three of us were a real family. Thanks to the healthy cynicism regarding marriage any child of divorce should have, I wasn't in a rush to get married, but I could see us heading that way someday.

But "Happily Ever After" is too boring for a Manic Pixie Dream Girl.

The blowups became more frequent. Small incidents like my not getting a sketch she wrote or asking an (I thought) innocent question about a job interview would set her off. The fights often escalated into an indictment of our entire relationship. As we approached our three-year anniversary, things got worse. Kelly was laid off from her day job and when employment leads dried up, a bout of depression set in. I paid extra bills and tried to stay positive, but telling her "Everything's going to be all right" no longer worked. She became withdrawn, quiet, and cold. We stopped having sex and she took up smoking cigarettes for the first time since I'd known her. But I didn't consider breaking up. I held to the belief that her reservations were about her insecurities, not our relationship. This was "true love," which meant every pain was worth enduring, every issue worth fixing. Even if one of the issues was my partner telling me she didn't want to be with me. I wouldn't let something subtle like that dissuade me. I just needed to love harder, to fix more.

But we hadn't hit rock bottom yet.

One night, I awoke at 3:30 a.m. to find Kelly hadn't come home or called. She wouldn't pick up her phone and with each call I grew more upset, vacillating between worry and anger. I hated Voicemail-

Greeting-Kelly for acting so perky when she KNEW I was incensed. The real Kelly, clearly drunk, finally answered at almost 5:00 a.m.

"Why didn't you call me?" I asked.

"I forgot," she said and offered no further explanation.

"Do you want me to come pick you up?"

"No, I'm still having fun, I'll just crash here," she said as she hung up.

I didn't know where "here" was. As I put down the phone, I realized I'd been hoping she was in trouble—at least then I'd have a problem to solve. But she didn't need or want my help.

The next morning she came home around 9:00 a.m., and her lack of balance revealed she hadn't yet crossed from drunk to hungover. I questioned her about her night, but I was more disapproving parent than angry lover, playing my role of the rational, square boyfriend. She offered a perfunctory apology and went to sleep.

This pattern repeated itself often. At night she played the Manic Pixie Dream Girl for other people, during the day I got the Hungover Depressed Pixie Nightmare. She explained her behavior by saying she was going through a rough patch and needed space.

At the end of the summer I went on a camping trip to Lake Powell with friends, thinking it would be good to have a little time apart. Before I left, I wrote Kelly a letter in which I acknowledged for the first time that our relationship might be unstable. But I also asked her to consider that this could be a temporary rough patch worth riding out. I ended with this paragraph:

I know this letter won't fix anything. Change will take time. But I still needed to write it, to let you know how much I love and care

for you. I know my love can't fix what's wrong, but I want you to
know it's here just the same, and it always will be.

I left the letter on her desk with a bouquet of flowers.

———

I spent the half-day drive to Lake Powell waiting for her to call, but the phone sat in the cupholder silent for hours and hours, miles and miles. Late in the afternoon it finally beeped—not a call, but a text message. She thanked me for the flowers but didn't mention the letter.

When I said in my letter that my love couldn't fix her depression, I was lying. I TOTALLY thought my love could fix EVERYTHING. That letter was my Grand Romantic Gesture, the one that saves the relationship and the girl. It was my Lloyd Dobler moment, holding a boom box over my head and blasting "In Your Eyes." In the movies the romantic gesture always works, but it failed me in real life. This was like Diane Court coming to the window only to shut it so she could go back to sleep. I gave her my heart; she thanked me for the $12.99 flowers.

I drove back to LA a few days later smelling of campfire and knowing my relationship was probably over. When I got home, Murray ran up to me with her tail wagging; Kelly barely looked up from her movie. I stood at the door, bag in hand, waiting for her to say something about the letter. If it couldn't save the relationship, she had to at least acknowledge it existed, right? But she said nothing. A week later, Kelly still hadn't mentioned the letter and neither had I.

"What's going on with us?" I asked one morning while she made coffee.

"I told you," she said, "I'm just having a hard time right now."

She tried to leave the kitchen, but I stepped in her way.

"That's not a good enough answer anymore."

She stared at me with her big eyes, the same eyes that had been filled with so much affection three years earlier when she'd told me she loved me for the first time. Now they just looked tired.

"I'm going to move in with my brother," she said.

"Temporarily?"

"No."

"But we got a puppy together," I said.

I let the statement hang in the air, as if it explained away everything. We'd only gotten Murray four months earlier—who gets a puppy with someone they want to dump? A puppy's not like a child; you can't have one by accident. No one has too much wine, pulls out late, and ends up with a puppy. A puppy is a choice. As recently as four months ago she'd CHOSEN for us to get a dog, which meant she'd believed in there being an "us."

The problem with this logic was that Kelly didn't abide by logic. She'd wanted a puppy so she'd gotten a puppy, and now she didn't want to be with me so she wasn't going to be with me. I was trying to explain away her emotions, but the ploy didn't work anymore. No longer all in on me, Kelly was all out. She left that day. My love couldn't "fix" her, and even worse, she didn't want to be fixed. Needing to be fixed is rule number one for being a Manic Pixie Dream Girl—how could she ignore it? I don't know, but she did, leaving our story to end not with credits rolling, but with crying and the division of possessions. I kept the dining room chairs and puppy; she kept the old-timey typewriters.

———

We've all had our heart broken. This book is about what happened to me after that heartbreak. And brunch. This book is also about brunch.

Part I

YOU TOO
CAN BE A
CASUAL DATER

1

A BRIEF HISTORY
OF MY LOVE LIFE

At the age of thirty, I was single for the first time in three years, though it might as well have been a decade. Here's a brief look at my dating history to show you what I mean.

Age: 0–13
Girlfriend: John Elway (Quarterback for the Denver Broncos)
Description: Prepubescent and blissfully uninterested in sex or girls, my attention was focused mainly on my sports hero. It was a very clearheaded time in my life.
Length of Relationship: 13 years

Age: 13–18
Girlfriend: My Hand (and Various Pillows)
Description: I discovered masturbation. It was spectacular. I had few dates, fewer kisses, and no girlfriends, but my friend masturbation was always there for me.
Length of Relationship: 5 years (Admission—we still see each other quite a bit.)

Age: 18–22

Girlfriend: Maria (First Love)

Description: We met during college orientation and dated for all four years of school. She was my first girlfriend and it was a wonderful relationship that only ended because neither of us wanted to marry the first person we'd dated.

Length of Relationship: 3.5 years

Age: 22–23

The Slump

Description: I didn't date or have sex with anyone for over a year. I'd gotten a girlfriend in college so quickly I hadn't figured out how to interact with girls well.

Length of Slump: 1.5 years

Age: 23–25

Girlfriend: Samantha (The One I Wasn't Ready for)

Description: Samantha was beautiful, kind, and a good girlfriend, but I was too immature to be a good boyfriend. I moved to New York City without her but didn't have the courage to end the relationship. We did long-distance for six months before I broke up with her over the phone because I had a crush on someone else.

Length of Relationship: 2.5 years

Time Single: Three weeks

Age: 25–27

Girlfriend: Ann (The Rebound)

Description: My crush on Ann finally made me end my relationship with Samantha. We dated for over a year and a half without saying I love you once (more on this later). I stayed in the relationship six months longer than I should have because I didn't want to hurt her feelings.

Length of Relationship: 1.5 years

Time Single: 72 hours (seriously)

Age: 27

Girlfriend: Melanie (The Friend)

Description: I'd known Melanie since high school and there'd always seemed to be a mutual attraction, but we were never simultaneously single. Three days after I broke up with Ann, while back home for Christmas, Melanie and I hooked up. Our passionate, but rocky, three-month, long-distance relationship ended with her dumping me because she loved me as a friend, but not romantically.

Length of Relationship: Three months

Time Single: Three months

Age: 27–30

Girlfriend: Kelly (Manic Pixie Dream Girl)

Description: You know ALL about this one already.

Length of Relationship: Three years

As you can see, I was a Serial Monogamist, with the condition at its peak between ages twenty-three and thirty. During that seven-year period, I dated four girls and was single for four months total, an average of five weeks per breakup. Like a monkey afraid to let go of one branch before grabbing the next, I swung from girl to girl, often having my next love interest in sight before the present relationship ended.

I became this way because I was the classic "Nice Guy." Nice Guys only date seriously. They are not the type to seduce a girl at a bar and take her home to fuck (not least because we don't "fuck"; we "make love"). Nice Guys don't "pick up" women. Instead, we meet them through a mutual friend or an adult learning class and send respectful Facebook messages asking if the girl would like to get dinner, or whatever, at a time totally convenient for her, if it sounds fun, NO PRESSURE. And if a Nice Guy succeeds in getting a date, we immediately aim for a relationship, not a fling. *A drunken makeout? Not without a promise ring, thank you very much.*

Once I had a girlfriend, I'd usually keep them for a long time, because Nice Guys make great boyfriends. I rarely raised my voice, didn't complain much, always remembered birthdays, gave massages, and got along with families. I preferred monogamy and never longed for the days of being single. Those days meant talking to strangers—I hated those days.

So what's wrong with being this fantastic-sounding Nice Guy? We're more concerned with seeming "nice" than actually being kind. Being nice means behaving in a way you think will make people like you. Kindness means being emotionally honest, even if it will make someone angry. The Nice Guy isn't good at being emotionally honest, and I was a prime example.

Much too worried about what other people thought of me, I wouldn't break up with a girlfriend when I wanted to because that was "mean" and I couldn't bear the idea of anyone not liking me. This is how you end up saying things like "I just want to get set up in New York on my own before you come."

If, on the other hand, my girlfriends wanted to break up with me, I'd try to convince them to stay, no matter the state of the relationship, because getting dumped felt like a statement about my inherent worth. I'd avoid or quickly diffuse confrontation, rather than solve the underlying issues. Being in a relationship was more important than being in the right relationship.

So, that's the problem with a Nice Guy. But how did I become one? How does anyone develop a definitive and crippling personality trait? Middle school, of course.

———

As a teenager, one of my nicknames was "Porcelain Baby Matteson." Puberty didn't hit for me until almost eighteen, so before college I weighed less than 130 pounds, was hairless from the neck down, and sported the smooth, youthful face of a wet porpoise. Friends would greet me in the hall by saying, "For three easy payments of $19.99, you can own your very own Porcelain Baby Matteson, complete with sun parasol."

While this weak, miniature body was good for a laugh, it wasn't great for my confidence, especially when it came to women. I wasn't terminally shy and I did have friends, but the idea of interacting with girls romantically terrified me. To me, sex and dating were like going to the moon—I knew people had done it, but I didn't understand the science behind it and part of me believed the whole thing might be a hoax.

Instead of asking a girl out, which would insinuate I liked her and saw her in a sexual way (disrespectful), I became the guy who made my friends' girlfriends laugh and then played video games in the basement while they made out. The guy who saw an invitation to study with a girl as that and only that. Too "nice" to ever make a move, I watched the jerks get the girls.

I first noticed the Jerk-Gets-the-Girl phenomenon in seventh grade, when every day in the halls I'd see some boy snap a girl's bra, plucking the strap so it made a loud *Slap!* Why were these girls letting the boys do this? Why weren't they reporting this behavior to the principal, the police, or the CEO of Victoria's Secret? Somebody?

The girls didn't even seem to be offended by this entry-level S&M. In fact, the boys doing the snapping were getting the girlfriends and, if the legends were to be believed, doing something to them with their fingers EVEN MORE disrespectful than the bra snapping.

How could girls like these jerks? I thought. *Why aren't they drawn to me, the nice guy who respectfully ignores them?*

At the time, I assumed girls looked past me because they had an inherent sense I'd be insufficient as a boyfriend. Much later, I realized that while bra snapping was a disrespectful and juvenile interaction, it was, at least, an interaction. And dating requires interaction.

In order for me to make an advance on a girl, I would have needed her to write me a letter (preferably notarized) explaining she liked me and was granting permission to kiss her. And even then I'd want to have my lawyer present at said contractually agreed upon kiss.

Things didn't get better in high school as I maintained my distance from women out of respect (fear). The closest I came to a relationship was an ongoing friendship with a girl I had a massive crush on. Sara smiled at me a lot, touched my arm sometimes, and laughed at my jokes, but, as one of the nicest people in school, she kind of did those things with everyone. I hid my feelings for her because I didn't want to be the idiot who mistook general kindness for a sign of interest. *Oh, she said hello and treated me like a regular human being—I could have sex with her!*

Sara and I hung out a lot the summer after our senior year. One night, propped up by liquid courage (Dr Pepper—I didn't drink in high school), I asked if she'd like to go up to the reservoir and listen to music. While this may sound innocent enough, people didn't go up to the reservoir to assess the quality of the town's drinking water. This was our "makeout point."

"That sounds great," she said.

"Cool, yeah, whatever, let's do that, just an idea," I said, hoping to convey I made out with girls all the time, rather than never in history.

I stayed silent as I drove up the winding road to the reservoir, afraid saying anything could cause Sara to change her mind. We parked and gazed out at the beautiful, clear night. The lights of the city stretched out below us, a mirror of the stars above.

To PERFECTLY set the mood, I put on a Dave Matthews Band CD (oh, everyone liked them back then, leave me alone), and for the next two hours we got buuuuuuusy . . . discussing various topics like our favorite foods. Why selfishly make out, when we could do humanity the service of deciding the pizza vs. cheeseburger argument once and for all?

Yes, all signs pointed to Sara being interested in me, but she hadn't sent me that notarized letter saying it would be okay for me to kiss her, so I was still nervous. She was so close I could smell her cherry ChapStick, but the three feet between our lips might as well have been a million miles. How would I get from here to there? The idea that I could just lean in and kiss her was ludicrous—she'd see it coming. No, I needed a ruse of some sort. Maybe I could propose a short-distance staring contest? Ask to practice CPR? Offer her a taste of the gum I was chewing?

I thought and thought and thought, but I could not come up with a "move." How did people do this? How was the human race thriving on Earth when kissing, forget full-on mating, was impossible?

"We'll need to leave pretty soon," Sara said near midnight, "so I can get home before curfew."

She may have hoped a deadline would spur some action on my part. It did not. Instead of kissing her, I immediately started the car.

"Well, we better get you home, then!" I said, relieved I no longer had to sit there failing.

I never did kiss Sara, or anyone else, during high school. On my personal map of life, sex was a blank space where, instead of information, it just said, "Here Be Dragons."

———

Things took a turn for the better after I left home, thanks to the magic of college orientation. At the new school I was a blank slate, no longer Porcelain Baby Matteson, the guy who hadn't kissed a girl. (I still somewhat resembled a porcelain baby doll, but at least no one knew that was like *my thing*.) It also helped that for the first two weeks of school, we were all going CRAZY. There was no parental supervision, no curfew, and a ready supply of alcohol.

It was like taking a bunch of rabbits in heat and throwing them into a pen together. And also those rabbits are drunk on Captain Morgan.

During this perfect storm of anonymity and promiscuity, I met my first girlfriend, Maria, a pretty midwestern girl. We were just friends for a few weeks, leading me to assume I'd be playing my normal supporting role with little screen time and almost no dialogue, but one night she asked if she could come to my dorm room to watch a movie.

Because my only furniture, an inflatable chair, couldn't hold two people, Maria and I had to lie next to each other in my tiny single bed as we watched the film *Tommy Boy* (Do I know romance or what?). I couldn't believe it. At college only a month and a girl was IN MY BED and our LEGS WERE TOUCHING. Not quite a notarized letter, but even I saw this as a green light. It still took all the way until the credits for me to do anything, though. As the film faded to black, I knew I was running out of time, so I abandoned any hope of pulling off a "move," practically flopping on top of her as I pushed my lips toward her mouth. To my amazement, she kissed me back. Turns out desperation can be a move.

We became an official couple soon after and I made up for lost time on the kissing front. Maria and I made out whenever we got a chance: between classes, after lunch, before bed, during movies, and when alone in an elevator. Because we were both virgins and not ready for sex, kissing was all we did. We'd make out for hours at a time, until our chins were red and chapped, our hair a mess, and our underwear fully wedgied from dry humping.

After a couple months we'd nearly worn through the crotches

of our jeans, so we decided we should go all the way. Losing our virginity to each other, as first loves, felt perfect, but I was nervous. Abstinence-focused Sex Ed had left me woefully unprepared for what happened during intercourse. I barely understood what a clitoris was. I knew it was part of the vagina and if you answered its three riddles it would grant you a wish, but that was about all.

Even buying condoms for the first time terrified me. I worried that Porcelain Baby Matteson would go into the store and say, "One box of sexual condoms, please," and the clerk would laugh. "Oh, no, I can't sell you those. Not only are you too young to have sex, but I can tell you're also not cool enough."

I put off the purchase until the afternoon of our planned virginity-losing ceremony. Once inside the drugstore, I found the condoms aisle, but actually stopping and picking a brand mortified me, so I kept walking, glancing over as I passed the section, trying to glean what I could. I did this several times, taking laps through the aisle, getting a little bit of information with each loop.

Lubricated? I thought the vagina took care of that, kind of like a self-cleaning oven. Ribbed for her pleasure? Sounds pretty good. Let the condom do some of the work and take the pressure off me.

After a few passes, I picked a box, but I needed to purchase something else, so I wouldn't look like some sort of deviant only there to procure sex supplies. But what to buy? I was a little thirsty—how about a beverage? *I'm just a normal sexually active guy trying to quench his thirst.*

I went to the cooler, scanned over my options, and chose . . . apple juice. Yep, I picked the beverage of choice for four-year-olds in order to make my shopping seem more adult. At the time it seemed like a great choice and I strode proudly to checkout thinking, *Matteson, you clever bastard, you've solved it!*

At the register, I found another trial—the woman doing checkout looked like a grandma. Not a normal grandma, either, but a cute one who would go by "MeMa" or something. I did not want to buy condoms from MeMa, but I'd come too far to turn back (I'd already opened the apple juice).

I approached the register and set my products on the counter. MeMa rang up the apple juice first. It went fine. She didn't suspect a thing. I don't know how she reacted to the condoms, because as she picked them up I was reading a package of gum and forcing a look of fascination onto my face to really sell it. *Huh, only two calories per piece. I would have guessed three.*

"Eighteen thirty-six is your total," MeMa said.

I slid my twenty-dollar bill across the counter, careful not to make any sudden moves, aware "the deal" could go south at any moment.

"And one sixty-four is your change," she said as she handed it back, playing it totally cool, as if she hadn't just sold me something that would later be worn on my penis.

"Have a nice night," she said as I headed for the door.

Lady, I've got a box full of condoms and a bottle of apple juice—you KNOW I'm about to have a good night.

———

Because Maria and I both had roommates, we checked in to a hotel room for our special night. You'd think that after years of looking forward to sex, we'd rip each other's clothes off, but we didn't.

Instead, we sat on the edge of the perfectly made hotel bed, both of us fidgeting silently. Some booze probably would have helped loosen things up, but as we were under twenty-one, the daiquiris we'd had with dinner were appropriately virgin.

When we finally got started, it didn't go smoothly. In the movies, having sex is easy. The guy gets on top of the girl, music plays, just the right amount of sweat appears on their brows, their butts are somehow tan, and they not only orgasm together, but that orgasm provides a clue to the mystery they're trying to solve.

In real life, we couldn't even get started. I'd thought it would be kind of like two magnets, that once our equipment got close enough they'd automatically pull together. Nope. I was thrusting blindly, as if I were playing an easy-looking carnival game that is actually impossible. And neither of us knew we could use our hands down there. I guess we thought sex had the same rules as soccer.

Finally, we managed to make it work, but a couple minutes in, Maria mumbled something. I couldn't make out what she'd said, but I assumed it was something sensual. After all, we were in the middle of some sensual sex.

"What did you say?" I whispered.

"Stop moving. It hurts."

I froze. We stayed that way, with me balancing on top of her, trying to not breathe, for three or four minutes, before she asked if we could stop completely. I rolled to the side. Had what we'd done counted? Was I no longer a virgin? As I pondered this, Maria started to cry.

"What's wrong?"

"That's just not how I thought it would go," she sobbed. She described what she'd expected, using the word *magical* more than once. I told her it would get better, reassuring myself as much as her.

The next morning, with the pressure of the first time gone, we had a much more successful go. But we did make one rookie mistake—we'd forgotten to put out the Do Not Disturb sign, probably because we'd never done anything in a hotel room worth disturbing before.

Right in the middle of our beautiful (awkward) deflowering, we heard a knock, followed immediately by the door opening. In walked a woman pulling a vacuum behind her.

"Please don't come in, we're busy!" I yelled. I would have been less embarrassed if she'd caught me chopping up a body.

"Sorry!" she said as she dashed out of the room. After the trouble of getting a hotel room, we were still walked in on.

Despite the interruption, we finished the deed. I don't know if it was magical, but there wasn't any crying, so I considered that a win. I was grinning for the rest of the day and wanted to stop everyone I passed and say, "Sex sure is great, right? I know, because I do sex. I'm a sexer. Feel free to discuss sex with me."

Maria and I were nearly inseparable throughout the rest of college. We did a semester in Paris together, a spring break in Cancún, and alternated Christmases at each other's houses. It was a great four years, but as graduation approached we realized we hadn't made a plan for how we'd be together postcollege. She was moving back home and I wanted to go to Alaska to work for the summer. Though it was clear we would break up, we decided not to do it until the end, so we could enjoy our last weeks of college together.

The morning after collecting our diplomas, we hugged goodbye as her cab idled in the street. The hug lasted long enough to make me wonder if leaving the only person I'd ever loved was the right decision. As her cab pulled away, she waved out the window and the tears that had been threatening to fall bullied their way out of my eyes.

Though I had a wonderful summer in Alaska, I disliked being single again. Splitting up had felt like the right thing to do, but I missed Maria and the intimacy I had with her, missed the validation I got from having a girlfriend who told me she loved me. It took more than a year to find my next girlfriend (The Slump) and I hated every minute of being single. I didn't know it at the time, but this was the beginning of the Nice Guy Cycle. My self-worth became so tied to having a partner that being single made me feel like a loser and getting dumped didn't mean one person didn't love me, it meant I was inherently unlovable. Thus, why I hung on to my relationship with Kelly, the Manic Pixie Dream Girl, so long.

But now I wanted to stop the Nice Guy Cycle. No more jumping from relationship to relationship. No more fear of being alone or hiding feelings to avoid confrontation. I wanted to have independent self-worth derived outside of a relationship. I had no idea HOW I would accomplish that, but I knew the first step—getting over my ex.

2

HOW TO GET OVER A BREAKUP

The small, homemade valentine card, made from red construction paper and white lace, said, "You're Swell!" on the outside, while a long note from Kelly about how much she loved me filled the inside. I took a deep breath to hold back the tears. What was sadder, that the words were untrue, or that she (and I) had believed them to be utterly true so recently? I tossed the card into a trash bag filled with other mementos from our relationship, a time capsule of happier days.

I'd found the keepsakes as I was packing to move out of the apartment we'd lived in together. If that wasn't sad enough, the day before, I'd had to go to a wedding in San Diego, my stepbrother's, a last-minute courthouse ceremony because his bride was from France and they needed to start the immigration paperwork as soon as possible. At least that's what they claimed. I knew the truth: they'd rushed the engagement to rub their joy in my face. Don't get me wrong, I was happy for my brother, but having recently been dumped, I viewed the wedding with a jaded eye, thinking, *We'll see if this lasts. They're young and getting married quickly. And also, love is not real.* Long skeptical of marriage, my breakup had further disillusioned me.

Making matters worse, I hadn't yet told some family members about my split, so I kept getting the question "Where's Kelly today?"

What I'd say—"We broke up a couple weeks ago."

What I wanted to say—"I have no goddamn clue where she is because we're no longer together. She doesn't love me anymore, despite the fact we got a puppy, so I'm alone today. But enough about me, let's talk about something emotionally crippling in your life."

———

Though I would come to love living alone (I make a good roommate for myself), it felt crushingly desolate at first. Having no one to eat with made cooking joyless. I stopped watching the sitcom *Parks and Recreation,* because Kelly and I had watched it together and the theme song had a Pavlovian effect, causing me to tear up within a few notes. At night, without another person in my bed, I felt like the sole survivor of a shipwreck, floating alone in a sea of blankets, my rescue doubtful. I quickly tossed aside my rule against Murray sleeping in the bed and discovered that a dog's coat is remarkably good at absorbing tears.

I didn't just come home to an empty apartment, either; I was in an empty apartment all day because I worked from home. While I tried to make it as a writer, working on screenplays and TV scripts in my spare time, I made money working for a company that sold office furniture. Finding stocks of used office cubicles to buy and resell wasn't exactly exhilarating enough to make me forget my failed relationship. I needed to be proactive if I was going to pull myself together.

I came up with an eight-step program:

1. Initiate Ghost Protocol—Act as if Kelly were a Mission: Impossible operative who'd been captured: disavow all knowledge of her and remove any evidence of her existence. I threw away pictures, unfollowed her on Twitter and Facebook, and hid her name in Gchat.

2. Mourn her as if she were dead—It was okay to miss Kelly, just like it's okay to miss a loved one who's passed away, but holding out hope of getting back together would be like waiting for a dead person to return from the grave. I kept in mind that attempting to contact the dead is crazy and trying to have sex with them even worse.

3. Listen to a lot of Billy Joel—I made "She's Always a Woman" by Billy Joel my official break-up theme song. Anytime I felt low, I'd listen to it on a loop, singing along with every lyric. This song is amazing because it feels like it's written specifically about your ex. *My girlfriend was frequently kind and suddenly cruel—how did you know, Billy Joel?*

4. Create a "regret fantasy"—I used my pain and anger as inspiration to work harder and be better, so one day Kelly would regret having let me go. I looked decades into the future and saw her on her deathbed, saying with her last breath, "I shouldn't have dumped you. It was the greatest mistake of my life." "Yeah, it was," I'd say, before hanging up so I could go back to enjoying my space vacation, which in this fictitious future I'm rich enough to be able to afford.

5. Turn depression into a great bod —There are few exercise routines as effective for losing weight as the I'll Show You workout plan. Especially when paired with the I'm Too Depressed to Eat diet.

6. Fill up the social calendar—With some planning, I could be too busy to be sad. I started hanging out with people I didn't have time for previously, my JV friend squad. Sure, I'd stop seeing them as soon as a new relationship started, but for now, I'd pretend I actually valued them.

7. Hate all things romantic—I began trashing all movies, books, shows, and songs about love. I would decry their hypocrisy and shout about their lack of realism. I'd pity any friend in a new relationship, telling them "Good luck with that." I became a warrior of truth, exposing love for the disease it was, a virus invented by Hallmark.

8. Talk about the breakup incessantly—I'd mull over the same things again and again, revisiting the reasons Kelly was wrong/stupid and why she shouldn't have left me. No matter the temptation, I would NOT ask friends about how they were doing, knowing it was important for my mental health to talk only about myself.

Grant, a former roommate and one of my best friends, was one of the people who had to endure step eight the most.

You know when something crazy or cool happens and you think, *That kind of thing only happens to other people*—Grant is the person it happens to. He's tall, athletic, good-looking, plays guitar, is a lot of fun, and random amazing things seem to happen to him regularly, particularly when it comes to women. On a weekend trip to Paris for business he hooked up with a French model, who then visited him in New York for a week of sex. Another time he met a friend of a friend through Facebook and ended up in a short-lived yet passionate long-distance romance. When a normal mortal randomly meets a woman online, she turns out to be a fifty-year-old dude who drives a truck in Ohio. In Grant's case, she was an NFL cheerleader. I would hate him if he weren't one of my best friends.

During one phone call, I made a rare exception to my "don't care about other people's lives" policy to hear about Grant's recent trip to Burning Man, a "counterculture festival" that takes place every year in August in the desert outside Reno. For one week, tens of thousands of people turn a dried-up lake into a pop-up town called Black Rock City. And shit gets weird. People band together in camps to create art pieces, bars, dance clubs, sex clubs, teahouses, libraries, restaurants, and anything else a town might need or want. The idea is to build an alternative society based on openness, sharing, and nonjudgmentalism. Sort of like summer camp for adults, but with way more patchouli.

Grant told me all about his experience: the great group of people he camped with and the parties they threw; the art; and the desert at night, every person, every car covered in LED lights, making the world look like a living Lite-Brite. He loved the sense of community and the change of perspective it afforded. Most important, he told me about how Burning Man was a very sexual place and featured many beautiful women wearing little clothing.

Grant had kissed scores of women during the week, sometimes without exchanging a word. He told me of the girl (another model, yawn . . .) he'd had sex with on top of a twenty-five-foot-high scaffolding platform while a party of hundreds raged below. Before he finished the story I blurted out, "I would like to go to Burning Man with you next year!"

Not only did I want to go to Burning Man, I wanted to do it all the way. I wanted to embrace the experience (have a lot of sex), explore the alternative society (have a lot of sex), discover things about myself (have a lot of sex), and do it all completely unfettered (so I could have a lot of sex).

In order to do that, though, I needed to be single when I went, and with Burning Man eleven months away, that meant going nearly a year without a relationship. This may not seem like a long time, but to a Serial Monogamist, it was daunting. It would be my longest single stretch in seven years.

I needed a plan.

3

BROS' BRUNCH

Growing up in Colorado, I didn't know about brunch. We only went out for breakfast twice a year, usually to commemorate either the birth or death of Jesus.

In Los Angeles, however, brunch is a lifestyle. Many Angelenos engage in this sacred tradition at least twice a month, sometimes waiting upward of an hour for a table so they can eat at the "right" place. After some time in LA, I got a handle on the differences between brunch and breakfast.

Breakfast—Meal lasts 30–40 minutes.

Brunch—Meal lasts 3–4 hours.

Breakfast—No alcohol.

Brunch—Bottomless mimosas.

Breakfast—Conversation about the weather or the price of gasoline.

Brunch—Conversations about your sex life, your friend's sex life, and your friend's friend's sex life. And *Mad Men*.

Breakfast—Attire: I don't know, whatever you put on when you get out of bed. Who cares, it's breakfast, not the prom.

Brunch—Attire: Men—aged jeans, a graphic T-shirt for an obscure band (preferably not yet formed), and sunglasses, which will remain on at all times, whether inside or out. Women—Two possible avenues: either tight-fitting, chic clothes suitable for an exclusive nightclub or an outfit so casual it could conceivably be worn by a midwestern pregnant woman binge-watching *One Tree Hill*. Wear nothing that falls between these extremes.

Breakfast—Food: Eggs over easy, hash browns, bacon, and sourdough toast. On a special occasion, like your birthday, you might order a Denver omelet.

Brunch—Food: A frittata with figs, applewood-smoked bacon, fresh goat cheese, and artisanal chives. A side of "fiesta hash browns" with fresh goat cheese. Just for fun, for the table, a stack of pumpkin walnut pancakes with Saigon cinnamon, real maple syrup, blanched bananas, fresh strawberries, and a dollop of crème fraîche. And a side of fresh goat cheese.

When Kelly and I broke up, my brunch habit kicked into high gear as I started getting together with two of my good friends, Kurt and Evan, almost every Saturday (and sometimes Sunday too). I went to college with Evan, and met Kurt through him. Evan is tall and wears glasses, portraying a mix of athleticism and bookishness that suits his personality, while Kurt is fit, with a boyish face. We became tight because we shared the three most important things when it comes to friendship—sense of humor, taste in pop culture, and a love of seasonal pancake toppings.

Every weekend we'd meet up, enjoy breakfast sweet-treats, and talk about relationships, dating, and feelings. Yes, we were basically acting out *Sex and the City*. As a writer and the main character in this book, I guess I'm Carrie, but I always felt the most affinity for Charlotte. Or whatever. Who knows, 'cause I've barely ever watched the show. Too busy watching football and shows about chopping wood.

Anyway, it was at a Bros' Brunch that I announced The Plan.

"I'm making a pact with myself to not have a girlfriend for a year, until after Burning Man," I said, between mouthfuls of avocado toast.

"That doesn't seem hard," Kurt said.

Kurt hadn't had a girlfriend in the two years I'd known him. It wasn't that Kurt couldn't get a girlfriend—he was funny, good-looking, and often successful with women—he just wasn't interested, content with the single life and spending time with family and friends. Like a veteran criminal used to solitary confinement, he scoffed at the minor stint of one year I'd have to serve.

Evan was, romantically speaking, the opposite of Kurt—he wanted nothing more than to be in a relationship, and he had a specific girl in mind. About a year earlier, a girl named Joanna had dumped him. Then they'd gotten back together. Then they'd broken up again. Then they'd gotten back together. And so on.

Kurt and I kept hoping Evan would move on, but he hadn't, even when Joanna relocated to Salt Lake City. We thought a seven-hundred-mile separation would be the death blow, but Evan wasn't so sure, pointing out that distance doesn't matter when it's True Love. (He would say stuff like this jokingly, but Kurt and I knew he was only half kidding.)

So, my goal to spend one year without a girlfriend didn't impress them. But that didn't mean it wasn't important. Not only would it leave me single to frolic at Burning Man, it would also be a chance to break my relationship pattern.

I'd decided that going quickly from one relationship to the next had been setting me up for failure. When driving stick, you have to downshift when you hit a red light; relationships should work the same way. Being in a loving, long-term relationship is like fifth gear and I hadn't been taking enough time off between women to get back to emotional neutral. I'd let a new relationship get serious right away, acting like a boyfriend from date one because I didn't know how else to act. A year off would allow me to start my next relationship fresh.

I hoped this strategy would help me find someone I not only loved, but who would be an objectively good life partner. Lust and infatuation had blinded me to objective incompatibilities in the past. In choosing partners, I'd been far too reliant on my "feelings," and my heart had proven to be a poor navigator, a Christopher Columbus type who claimed he'd found India just because he'd struck dry land.

Given my age, the next person I got serious with could become my wife, so I needed to pick wisely. To do this, I'd create a list of traits I wanted in a partner during my year of being single. By creating the list while single, I'd have a metric against which to measure future partners while in the throes of love.

Kurt took a bite of his French toast with quince and cardamom and considered how to respond to my airtight case.

"So, you're going to stay single for a year and think about what you want in a partner. Does that mean you're not going to have sex for a year?"

"No, I will be having a lot of sex," I said. "That's the second component of the plan—aggressive dating."

At the age of thirty I'd had sex with seven people, almost all serious girlfriends. I didn't know if this was a lot or a little, but either way, I wanted to diversify my experiences, to have casual sex, one-night stands, emotionless bangings, hookups, hook-downs, patty-cake parties, skin sessions, flip-digs, and other euphemisms I may have just made up. Were I a middle-aged white woman, this would be when I ate, prayed, and loved. Were I a middle-aged black woman, this would be when I got my groove back. As neither of those, this would be when I sowed my wild oats.

I would grab new experiences and go out with people I normally wouldn't consider. Anything was on the table, short of dating a vegan. This didn't mean I was planning on becoming a Pickup Artist, someone who went clubbing and owned flavored condoms. No, my aim was to date people respectfully, but without expectation of a relationship. By being up-front about my intentions, I'd get involved with like-minded people. I'd be a womanizer, but one of those nice womanizers that women love.

Evan stirred cream into his third cup of coffee (he has a problem) before he spoke.

"So, to fix the relationship problems you tend to have with women, you're going to have a ton of relationships with women?"

"Exactly! Instead of long-term, serious relationships, I'll have a string of noncommittal sexual relationships. By going against my normal dating pattern I'll figure out what I want in a partner."

"Wouldn't not dating anyone at all be a better way to do that?" Kurt asked. "Wouldn't that actually be the opposite of serial monogamy?"

He had a point.

"But then I wouldn't get to have all the sex," I said.

The Plan

1. Be single for a year.
2. Date and have no-strings-attached sex with a lot of women.
3. Hurt no one's feelings.
4. Develop a list of traits in an ideal partner.
5. Go to Burning Man and have crazy weird desert sex.
6. Use my list of traits to find my ideal mate.
7. Live forever in eternal bliss with my perfect wife.

Simple, logical, easy. The heart had its chance with romance. It was time for the brain to run the show.

I would take a little more time to mend before hacking through the dating jungle, but I set a target for my re-release into the wild: Halloween. The sluttiest holiday of them all would be an optimal time to debut "Single Matteson." Halloween was about five weeks away; by then I'd definitely be over Kelly. Or at least over her enough to have sex with a slutty Amelia Earhart or something.

4

BLACK SWAN

The party was at the Park Plaza Hotel, an Art Deco throwback that had long ago stopped being a hotel and now hosted events like these. We entered the grand marble lobby to find it transformed into a Halloween carnival, but I barely noticed the barker yelling through a megaphone or the freaks on stilts. Instead, I registered all the exposed flesh—long legs underneath naughty-schoolgirl skirts, cleavage escaping from black witches' corsets, and bare arms protruding from leotards. I'd chosen a good place to start being single again.

I went as a "dead cowboy," complete with toy arrows sticking out of my chest as if I had been shot by Indians. I figured the costume embraced the macabre spirit of Halloween, while still being sexy—who can resist the Marlboro Man? Kurt, my plus-one for the evening, dressed as Glenn Danzig from the Misfits, with a long black wig, fake tattoos, and a tank top.

There was one downside to the party—Kelly was going to be there. We'd bought tickets before the breakup and she'd let me know she was still attending. I dreaded seeing her, but at least it would be a good opportunity to further my ongoing quest to "win" the breakup.

After a relationship, it's not about recovering emotionally, it's about winning, and you win by seeming like you're doing better than the other person, even if you're not. If Kelly spotted me at the party making out with a slutty Eleanor Roosevelt, she'd think I'd moved on and I'd score major points in The Breakup Game, points I needed, because when you get dumped, you start way behind.

———

After a fruitless hour at the bar, Kurt and I wanted to try a new venue, so we made our way to the ballroom. The dance floor was populated with dead people, animals, movie characters, mythical creatures, and sexy professionals all dancing shoulder to shoulder, heads bobbing to the beat.

We were watching from the sidelines when I spotted Kelly. A jolt of energy burned through me as my fight-or-flight system reacted to the close proximity of a source of pain. When she caught sight of me we just stared for a moment, coming to terms with the fact that we couldn't pretend we hadn't seen each other. I gave her a meager wave. She walked toward me. Guess we would talk and be all adult about it. DUMB.

We spoke for a few minutes, careful to focus only on Murray, the party, and the cool costumes we'd seen. We'd had enough to say to one another to fill three years of a relationship, but now we struggled to fill three minutes. I was anxious for Kelly to leave so I could get back to not talking to the hot girls at the party.

As we hugged goodbye, Kelly violated our unspoken agreement not to speak of the breakup.

"You doing okay? Everything okay? It's hard, right? It's been hard. Aw. Anyway. Hard. Yeah. Okay?"

"Yes," I said, "I'm okay."

I watched her leave the ballroom, happy she was going, but sad I was happy. The person I'd valued most in my life had become the one I least wanted to see.

———

Strengthened by another whiskey and Coke, and with renewed purpose after having seen Kelly, I waded onto the dance floor. Kurt and I were separated now, both on our own missions. It was nearly 1:00 a.m. and time was running out.

After a few songs, I caught the eye of a woman dressed as the Black Swan. It was the fifth iteration of the costume I'd seen—the movie had come out that year—but the best one yet. She wore a beautiful handcrafted feather mask and a black leotard that showed off the body of someone who must have received a generous Barre Method gift card at some point.

We orbited each other until we were almost touching.

"Hi," I said, creative as always.

"Hi."

"Great party, right?" More A+ material.

"Yes," she said with a smile.

I tried to dance closer, but one of the arrows sticking out of my chest poked her in the breast. My costume was getting more action than I was. She giggled and flicked the arrow away as I apologized.

We couldn't talk much over the music, so we mostly just danced. I reached out and touched her arm. She didn't pull away, so I moved in closer. My arrows and her tutu prevented us from dancing straight on, so instead we stood nearly side to side, with our hips touching like we were doing a dance from the '50s called the Hip-Whip or something.

The dance floor around us thinned as people went home, but we stayed till the end. Eventually, the overhead lights came on, revealing a floor littered with dropped tails, bloody axes, and other random bits of costume.

"Can I walk you out?" I asked.

"Yes."

As we shuffled toward the exit, I hoped Kelly was still in the room and could see me leaving with someone. You only earn points in The Breakup Game if your ex sees the scoreboard.

The cool air was a welcome reprieve as we emerged into the night. People stood around smoking and talking as they waited for their rides. The smell of bacon-wrapped hot dogs, the official late-night street food of LA, filled the air.

"I'm that way"—Black Swan pointed—"on the other side of the park."

I took her hand and we walked in the direction she'd indicated. As we passed a trash can, I removed my arrows and tossed them in so they wouldn't interfere with the kiss I hoped was about to happen.

"My car's on this block," she said as we crossed a street, "but we could take a walk around the lake."

She pointed to a lake down the hill in the park, illuminated by the moon and framed by the lit-up buildings of downtown Los

Angeles. For weeks I'd hoped this night would result in a romantic rendezvous like this, but I knew it couldn't happen. Though there are few physiological compulsions stronger than the sex drive, the urge to urinate is one of them. It had been several hours and several drinks since I'd last gone to the bathroom and my bladder was being a real cock-block.

"Ah, no, it's late, we should get home," I said. "But it was great to meet you. Could I give you a call?"

"I'll talk to you soon, I hope," she said as she put her number into my phone.

I leaned in for a kiss.

I should have been reveling in this perfect little moment, a cowboy kissing a ballerina beneath a streetlight, but instead I was focused on not peeing my pants. The top half of me was dedicated to Black Swan, but below the belt I was doing the pee-pee dance, rubbing my knees together to maintain control.

Convinced I'd made a sufficient impression, I pulled away and offered the traditional goodbye of Los Angeles: "Drive safe." (Which really means "Good luck with the drunk driving.")

As soon as her car was out of sight, I sprinted toward the nearest tree in the park, struggling to get to my fly as I ran. The unfamiliar chaps proved hard to navigate (how did people pee in the Old West?) but I did manage to avoid pissing my pants.

Back at the party exit, I found Kurt sitting with a girl dressed as Mystique from *X-Men*, her body and face covered in blue paint, a bit of which was smeared on Kurt's chin. We'd both had a successful night.

When I got home, I stripped out of my cowboy clothes and

went straight to bed, but before I fell asleep, I pulled up Black Swan's contact file. I'd gotten a number. I'd kissed a girl. I'd done it.

———

As I knocked on Black Swan's door to pick her up for our first date, I realized I hadn't seen her face unmasked. What if it turned out she had a great body, but a face like Paul Giamatti? My heart started beating a retreat, but it was too late to back out.

The door opened and there stood a woman who looked nothing like the great American character actor. Her porcelain-white skin, angular facial features, and precisely parted hair lent her a fine quality, as if she were from the upper reaches of French aristocracy.

We went to an artisanal pizza place in Echo Park, a hip neighborhood in Los Angeles, and as we walked inside she expressed her approval.

"It's a great little place," I said, not mentioning it was my first visit and I'd only found the place after two hours of internet research. No woman has ever said, "Your mastery of Yelp is melting my panties."

The first-date small talk was much harder than I would have expected. We discussed work—she had a job. We discussed movies—she saw them. We discussed childhood—she'd been a child. Long periods of silence punctuated each topic as I struggled to come up with something else to say. Our awkwardness reminded me we weren't on this date because of personality compatibility. She looked good in a leotard and I made a cute cowboy, so here we were eating overpriced pizza.

At the end of dinner the waiter set down the bill, and I grabbed it, ever chivalrous. With appetizers, drinks, entrées, dessert, tax, and tip, the total came to over $100. I hadn't considered how much casual dating would cost. Could I take out a small-business loan for trying to get laid?

Back at her place, we kissed good night on her doorstep, but it was a proper, by-the-book, sober, first-date kiss, way less passionate than the one we'd shared on Halloween. I drove back to my apartment knowing "It" was missing. We were two kind, polite, attractive adults, but we didn't have much chemistry. Still, that was okay—I wasn't looking for a girlfriend. I was looking for fun. By which I meant sex.

Our next couple of dates were variations on the first—stilted conversation over dinner followed by brief kisses to end the night. On the third date she invited me into her apartment, but we stayed just inside the door, making out standing up and wearing our coats. With my rate of progress, we'd make it down the long hall into her bedroom by the nineteenth date, at which point I'd be bankrupt. If I wanted casual sex, Black Swan was the wrong person to be dating, but, dedicated to my plan, I asked her out again anyway.

A few hours before our fourth date, I received a text message: *I'm sorry to cancel last-minute, but I met someone recently and I'd like to see where it goes, so I think it would be inappropriate for us to go out tonight.*

I'd been dumped! Or whatever you call it when the person you've dated three times decides not to see you anymore. Downsized? That's what it felt like. Due to a redundancy in my position, I was being let go.

From not getting laid to getting laid off, my first venture into casual dating was pretty much a total failure. It had been so unserious I hadn't even gotten a chance to tell her I wasn't looking for anything serious.

Despite the blow to my ego, I was thankful she'd told me this before the date and glad she'd texted instead of calling. In a serious relationship, a face-to-face breakup is necessary—don't text *Divorcing U. My lawyer will hit u up 4 alimony deets*—but in a brief, casual relationship, the text is the way to go. It's the instant death of a bullet to the brain, rather than the prolonged suffering of a botched hanging.

I texted back: *Totally understand. Thanks for being honest. Good luck.*

With my dating trial run out of the way, I was ready to get serious about nonserious dating. Halloween wouldn't happen for another year, though; I needed a new source for finding women. It was time for internet dating. I had been rejected by one woman, but I knew that with the power of the internet behind me, I could be rejected by MANY women.

5

OKAY, CUPID!

My first online date was with a woman named Angela. Her profile, full of references to NPR and comic books, had suggested she belonged to the "cute nerd" phylum, and her looks matched. She had long brown hair, a shy smile, and wore a lot of (somehow) flattering cardigans in her profile pictures.

After exchanging a few messages, we met up for a drink on a Friday night. For the first hour the date was pleasant, if not noteworthy, but then, in the middle of a discussion about the comic book *Y: The Last Man,* there was a pause in conversation and held eye contact, which led to us making out aggressively right there on our stools. As we kissed, her thumb caressed my inner thigh, and I put my hand up the back of her shirt.

Normally, I wouldn't be game for this level of PDA, but no one in this Hollywood dive seemed to mind. The group sitting behind us in the booth were too busy taking turns snorting coke in the bathroom to notice us and, besides, anything Angela and I were doing paled in comparison to the octogenarian in a mink coat lip-synching to "I'm Every Woman" as it blared from the jukebox.

After an hour of alternating between talking and kissing, we exited the bar and walked to her car. Though she was parked only three blocks away, the walk took forty-five minutes because we kept stopping to make out. It was during one of these passionate sessions, this one against the window of a closed Subway sandwich shop, that I thought, *Online dating is awesome!*

For our second date, Angela came to my apartment for a drink before dinner. The combination of a cute dog and a hand-shaken cocktail proved to be a powerful aphrodisiac—we were making out before she'd finished her Manhattan.

That would have been enough excitement for me, but we didn't stop there. We moved to the bedroom and had sex before we even went to dinner. Sex *before* the date. It was a concept I hadn't experienced before, but immediately I saw its merits—it was just like sex after the date, except sooner.

Having sex with a new partner was exciting but strange. Being intimate with someone besides Kelly was the final piece of evidence that our relationship was truly over, and that realization made me a little sad. Not sad enough to stop having sex, but still, a little sad. Despite my melancholy, the session was still fun, because as the saying goes, "Sex is like pizza—even when it's bad you still have an orgasm." (Maybe I've got that slightly wrong. I don't know. I really enjoy eating pizza.)

"Thanks for not waiting until after dinner," Angela said as we lay next to each other afterward.

She was thanking *me*? For sex? Men were supposed to thank women for sex, not the other way around, right? Growing up, I'd believed sex was something to be obtained from women, a gift they gave once the man had proven himself worthy and of noble intentions. This view of sex had more or less remained intact into my adulthood. While I knew women enjoyed sex, I felt men wanted it more, which meant it took time and skill to procure, like a reservation at a popular restaurant.

But I hadn't "earned" the sex with Angela. She'd wanted the sex as much as I had and my desire flattered her. There was no talk of it being "too soon" or of what it "meant." We wanted to have sex so we had sex. I hadn't thought casual dating would be this simple.

After dinner, we returned to my apartment and had sex again.

"I should probably get going," she said as she reached for her clothes.

"You're welcome to stay the night."

"Really? You're inviting me to stay over?"

It was a simple, polite gesture intended to save her a drive home at two in the morning. From the look on her face, you'd think I'd offered her the last of my water in the middle of the desert. If basic decorum impressed women, I would do well.

As we were falling asleep, Angela pulled in close for some cuddling. I froze. Having her head on my shoulder felt more intimate than intercourse. Once sufficient time had passed, I pulled away and turned my back to her, free to fall asleep on my side of the bed with a foot of sheets between us. I highly recommend a king-sized bed if you're going to be engaging in casual sex.

Angela and I went out one more time, but neither of us followed up. I think we both knew it wasn't heading anywhere. There was no breakup or explanation of why the relationship had stopped, because it hadn't been a "relationship" to begin with. We'd shared a few nice nights together and moved on with no hard feelings. In other words, online dating was awesome.

———

Though Angela was the first person from online I dated, she was not the first person I messaged. That honor belonged to a woman with Audrey Hepburn looks and the screen name LE-GAL81. Other than her groan-inducing screen name (she was a lawyer), her profile was as cute as her picture. She loved frozen yogurt, dogs, and hiking. I had a dog! That I sometimes took hiking! After enjoying frozen yogurt! I was smitten with my perfect match.

I obsessed over her profile, visiting it several times a day, and compulsively scrolling through her pictures. I wrote and rewrote my message to her, perfecting my hilarious (not hilarious) Trader Joe's anecdote. After probably the ninth draft, I sent the message to my digital dream girl. I didn't bother writing to anyone else because internet dating had already worked, matching me with my true love. OkCupid may have considered us an 84% match, but the universe had us at 100%.

Timeline of Thoughts after
Sending an Internet Dating Message

Day 1: Of course she hasn't written back. A same-day response would seem desperate.

Day 2: She wants to write back, but she's busy. That's good. I'm GLAD she hasn't responded yet—it means she has a life.

Day 3: She's probably overwhelmed by the beautiful prose in my message and moved by the amazing connection we have when it comes to ice-cream flavor favorites. She's taking her time with her response because she wants to get it right.

Day 4: No matter that she hasn't responded. Our relationship will last years, so who cares if it's delayed a few days?

Day 5: WHAT'S THIS GIRL'S GODDAMN PROBLEM?!

LE-GAL81 never wrote back and I took the rejection hard. Certainly she'd found something deficient about my profile and, by extension, me as a person. A week passed before I sent out more messages, but my mood quickly rebounded when I got a reply from a beautiful Spanish girl. She had long, voluminous hair, olive skin, and a perfect smile. But there was a catch. The Spanish girl turned out to be Evan's ex-girlfriend. Millions of girls online and I message one of my best friend's exes. Laura (pronounced with a rolled Spanish *r*) had actually gone to college with Evan and me (they dated senior year), but I didn't realize who she was because we hadn't seen each other in almost a decade. She didn't recognize me, either, until I mentioned where I went to school.

Omg dude. I went there too and we know each other! You dated Maria, who I had classes with, and I went out with Evan, and this is so awkward. Haha! Did you realize? Was this Evan's joke? Or did you not recognize me?

"Online dating for a month and you're already messaging my ex-girlfriends," Evan chided me the next time I saw him.

I assured Evan I wouldn't ask Laura out. It was a shame, because our initial exchange had been promising, but the look of relief on

Evan's face told me I'd made the right choice. Not only had Evan and Laura dated, they'd stayed friends and were still very close. Understandably, he didn't want two of the closest people in his life hooking up.

Some good did come from connecting with Laura, however. Once it was established we weren't going to date, Laura and I could openly talk about our dating experiences. Hearing a woman's perspective was helpful.

She told me she sometimes got DOZENS of messages in one day, many of them short, vulgar, and grammatically incorrect. (Come on, guys, it's not *I want to put my dick in YOU'RE pussy.*) Laura sometimes got so frustrated she would delete her whole inbox and start from scratch.

This information helped me understand that rejection, or more accurately, being ignored, was the norm when online dating, so I shouldn't take it personally. LE-GAL81's failure to return a message was probably more about the process itself than about me. Maybe she didn't respond because she was taking a break from dating. Maybe she accidentally deleted my message. Maybe she didn't even know how to read.

With this knowledge came courage. I began searching online profiles at all hours of the day, and the more time I spent online, the more efficient I became at finding good matches. Soon I could determine a woman's attractiveness based on a thumbnail picture alone. It's sad that this impressive skill has no real-world applications. *We know the bomber was the most attractive of these three suspects, but we only have one-inch by one-inch mug shots—can you help us, Matteson?*

I started to enjoy the process. OkCupid was like Facebook, except instead of seeing people I didn't like in high school, I saw profiles of women who theoretically would have sex with me. I considered this a significant upgrade from Facebook.

After the LE-GAL81 catastrophe, I dashed off only short messages. I wouldn't waste time on a missive that might get lost among *Luv dem tits, wan 2 fuck?* messages. The note didn't need to make the woman fall in love with me or communicate the essence of my being; it only needed to be intriguing enough to get her to my profile. A couple of times I simply sent *Do you like me? Check yes or no,* and it got a reply. Eventually my quantity-over-quality approach worked and I ended up in Makeout City with Angela, a success that turned out to be a sign of things to come.

6

THE TALK

There is a checklist you can use to determine if a date is going well.

- Is she sitting close to you?
- Is she laughing at your jokes?
- Is she initiating physical contact?
- Is she awake?

I had checked off the first three with a flourish, but not the fourth. Shortly after our second round of drinks arrived, Bridget's head fell forward like she was a trucker who had run out of speed. A quick recovery proved she hadn't passed out or had a "spell." She had just drifted off. In the middle of our date. During the climax of a story. It was good material too! Another date had found the story very amusing. And yet, it bored Bridget into unconsciousness.

"I'm so sorry," she said, "it's been a busy week at work and the wine went to my head a bit. You weren't being boring or anything."

"Oh, it's fine," I said, doing my best to hide my contused ego.

There was no good-night kiss, only more apologies. I assumed

I wouldn't be getting a second date—unless Bridget found herself suffering from insomnia—but she texted me the next day and asked when we could go out again.

For our second date I asked her to go on a hike in Malibu, which is about forty minutes outside Los Angeles. After I'd asked, I realized how potentially off-putting this date request might have been. *Hey, I know you barely know me, and you have a propensity to drift off, but why don't we go on a long car ride out of town and then walk into the wilderness where ~~no one can hear you scream~~ we can enjoy the outdoors.* I knew I wasn't going to serial-kill her, but she didn't know I wasn't going to serial-kill her. Still, Bridget said yes, perhaps thinking the only danger I posed was boring her to death.

The date ended up lasting almost eight hours, half of which we spent in horrible LA traffic. But Bridget, Murray, and I had a good time anyway. Once back in LA, I suggested we go to my place so I could cook her dinner. She agreed. (NOTE: If a guy offers to cook dinner for a girl it's not because he's a wannabe chef, it's because his kitchen is close to his bedroom.)

The tactic worked. Before I could so much as put water on to boil, we were in my bedroom, with Bridget taking point. Her sexuality was unabashed in a way I hadn't experienced. She instructed me where and how she wished to be touched, her actions indicating that my desires were a distant second to hers. I did nothing more than say, "Yes, ma'am," and do as I was told until Bridget finished loudly. Only then was it my turn. By the time I'd caught up she was ready to go again.

Did I mention online dating is awesome?

Over the next few weeks I went out with Bridget a few more

times and our compatibility in and out of the bedroom flourished to the point where I knew we'd soon have to have The Talk.

The Talk is when you define what you're looking for in a relationship, how you feel, and whether you want to be exclusive. I dreaded giving this State of the Union address because I didn't have good news for the country. I wanted to keep seeing Bridget (and sexing her), but I didn't want to be her boyfriend and I was sure this would hurt her. After all, we'd gone on several nice dates and I'm wonderful—how could she not be in love with me? I would have to be delicate during The Talk to make sure she wouldn't throw herself from a bridge upon learning she couldn't have me.

But, before I got the chance, Bridget had The Talk with me. (This is more or less the transcript from our online discussion, my thoughts added in parentheses.)

Bridget: *hey*
Me: *Hi.*
Bridget: *I think we're gonna have to slow it down for a bit*
i've been having a grand time, but i'm seeing other people too

(Okay, so she wasn't exactly picking out wedding china.)

Me: *that's okay*
I am as well

(Don't feel too proud of yourself. I'm a Player too. Playas gonna play.)

Bridget: *nice*

(Well, that seems a little patronizing.)

Bridget: *we've gotten to know each other better than I usually do so maybe in the future we could try again, but I'd like to leave it for now.*

(YOU'RE letting ME down easy? That's what I was going to do!)

Me: *If it makes it any easier I'm not looking for anything serious. I just enjoy your company.*
Bridget: *hmmm*
thinking. Haha
Me: *If you've gotten serious with someone, or aren't interested, no problem*
but if you're worried I'm trying to make you into my girlfriend, don't be

(No need to worry about me. I'm Mr. Chill-As-Can-Be Bachelor.)

Bridget: *i'm just thinking that hanging out is fun, and if it doesn't have to be something more serious then maybe we can still hang out*
i'm in an "open relationship"

(Well, well, well, the truth comes out.)

Me: *oh. so, you have a primary boyfriend, but you guys have*
an open relationship?
Bridget: *it's become that yes*
well i don't know

(Does her boyfriend know it's an open relationship?)

Me: *listen, I'm a pretty relaxed open person*

(Oh boy—starting a sentence with "listen" makes it sound like
I'm recruiting for a cult and ending it with "I'm a pretty relaxed
open person" makes it sound like orgies are a very large part of that
cult.)

Me: *I like spending time with you*
I like having sex with you
Bridget: *yea we were pretty good at that*

(Ego boosted! Date me or don't, I don't care—you said I'm
good at sex. That's all I need.)

Me: *I got out of a serious relationship a few months ago*
so I'm not looking to be anyone's boyfriend right now

(Girl, I'm a wolf, you can't domesticate me!)

Bridget: *ok*
yeah, i do like our dating thing

that's my goal right now too
to be open about my relationship
this could work.
Me: *cool. seriously don't stress.*

(Ugh, I sound like a guidance counselor who wants his students to think he's cool.)

Me: *Whatever you're comfortable with*
although I would like to be good at sex with you again soon
Bridget: *haha*
ok, we'll do that soon
well i've gotta go

And thus, for the first time in my life, I had a "Fuck Buddy."

Every three or four weeks we'd get together, share a meal or see a movie, and have sex. This arrangement seemed like magic to me. I knew I didn't have to "earn" sex anymore (thanks, Angela), but I still sort of thought, deep down, women ultimately wanted a serious relationship. They might say *Let's take things slow,* but that really meant *I hope this is the one who finally puts a baby inside me!* Of course I was wrong. Bridget wanted the same casual relationship I did.

Bridget and I got so comfortable, we could talk about the other people we were seeing and give each other advice. One weekend I even gave her a ride to a date. We'd spent a Saturday night together and in the morning I took her to the Farmers Market, an LA classic, where she was meeting another guy. We arrived a bit early, walked around, and ran into my friend Kathy.

"And who was that?" Kathy asked after Bridget had walked away.

"A friend."

"Friend, huh?"

"Yeah . . ."

"Come on," Kathy said, "you two look like raw sex. Did you fuck behind the kettle corn tent, like, five minutes ago?" Kathy, a petite girl in her twenties, cussed like someone four times older and twice as drunk.

"No. It was thirty minutes ago and in my bed."

"Where's she off to now?"

"She has a date."

"Oh, you little sluts," she said, and shook her head. Kathy and her boyfriend, Jason, had known me as the monogamous Nice Guy and my new MO amazed them.

"And you don't mind that she's seeing someone else?"

"No. She knows I'm seeing other people too. We're just honest about it."

"Well, aren't you so fucking goddamn adult."

Kathy was giving me shit, but I DID feel like a fucking goddamn adult. In some ways, my relationship with Bridget felt like the most grown-up relationship I'd ever had. There were no coded communications, passive-aggressive stabs, disappointments, or jealousy. We were two people who liked to have sex with each other and didn't pretend it was anything more. It was simple and honest, which wasn't true of some of my past "real" relationships. I now saw that with the right person, The Talk didn't have to end a relation-ship. This honesty thing, I realized, might be crazy enough to work.

———

The next time I saw Kurt and Evan, I reported my positive progress.

"The Plan is working—I am casual sexing and I haven't gotten a girlfriend or an STD."

"Yet," Kurt said, "you don't have an STD yet."

"Don't give up on yourself, buddy," Evan said, "you'll get one soon."

When our food arrived, we devoted a minute to our ritual prep-arations, cutting eggs, applying butter, dripping hot sauce. I took a few bites of my country potatoes dish (the brunch edition of hash browns), and looked at Evan.

"Okay, so let's hear it. How was Salt Lake City?"

He'd recently returned from visiting his ex, Joanna. Evan took a dramatic sip of his coffee.

"It started out really great. The first two days were amazing. Then, on the last night, she got weird and distant. Said she was overwhelmed by me being there."

"So, are you guys back together?" Kurt asked.

"You know, our relationship is too complex for labels. We're just trying to let it be whatever it is."

"Which is nothing?" I said.

"I wouldn't expect a slut like you to understand something as deep as what Joanna and I have."

He was kind of joking, but he was also right; I didn't understand what Evan had with Joanna. His breakup was so different from mine. They'd been (mostly) broken up for almost a year and Evan wasn't seeing anyone new. Only a few months removed from being with Kelly, I had had sex with multiple women, which meant I was unquestionably over her. Your penis doesn't work right if you're not over your ex. That's biology.

7

SEEING THE EX

After a pleasant dinner, my date, Sonya, and I headed to a comedy show. The person taking tickets looked familiar, but I couldn't remember how I knew him. Not wanting to insult him, I acted generically friendly, figuring his name would pop into my head shortly.

"It's great to see you, buddy," I said. "How are you?"

"Um, good," he mumbled. As he took my hand his eyes widened and his smile sagged a bit. This subtle fear response jogged my memory. I was shaking hands with Kelly's new boyfriend.

———

Three months after Kelly and I broke up, I stumbled upon (actively sought out) her Facebook page and saw she was "In a Relationship" with a guy named Ryan. Being "In a Relationship" on Facebook doesn't mean you've had a single date or gone out for a couple weeks—it means you're committed and exclusive. People say "I love you" more readily than they change that status. If Kelly had updated Facebook that quickly, it meant the new relationship must have started right after we split. Or even before.

Ryan was a part of the group of new friends Kelly often stayed out with all night toward the end of our relationship. Though he was more Kelly's friend than mine, I did know him and we'd even performed improv together on a few occasions.

One night during that period, when I tried to catch up with her after work, she was slow to respond to text messages, vague about where she was, and not answering calls. She seemed to be avoiding me. Finally, after I'd spent an hour eating alone in a diner, I'd gotten an address from her.

I'd expected to find a group at the bar, but it was only her and Ryan. They were sitting close together at a table and laughing loudly at a "bit" they were doing. They tried to describe the joke, but explanation always ruins humor, so I was Matteson, Destroyer of Laughter.

The loud music prevented me from hearing much from across the table, but I could tell from their body language the conversation was going really well. About halfway through my second drink a thought occurred to me—*I am crashing my girlfriend's date.* Despite being the boyfriend, I was the third wheel. Amazingly, my initial feeling was guilt. I felt bad for interrupting. *These crazy kids were having fun before I rained on their parade!*

When we got back home, I asked Kelly if anything was going on between her and Ryan. She denied it, saying they were just friends.

"Then why did I feel like I was interrupting a date?"

"It wasn't a date."

"A guy and a girl go out for dinner and drinks. That's what a date is. You were on a date."

"I was hanging out with a friend. Don't be so controlling. The way you were acting at the bar was embarrassing."

Our relationship should have ended that night. I should have pushed harder to find out what was going on with Ryan and, more important, us. This would have led to the truth about our crumbling relationship and we would have broken up. That's what should have happened. Instead, I immediately retreated from my position and apologized. Controlling, embarrassing, jealous? That's not me. I wasn't some chauvinist who wouldn't let his girlfriend have male friends. No, I was the Nice Guy who always understood and never made a fuss. Instead of standing up for my real feelings, I shoved them under an apology and our relationship carried on for another miserable month.

When I saw that Relationship Status update, I felt vindicated. I WAS RIGHT—there had been something going on! I wasn't a crazy, paranoid, controlling boyfriend; I had reacted appropriately to a weird social situation. The silver lining was thin, though, and I quickly became bummed. While our relationship was failing, Kelly had been forming a new one with Ryan. And I couldn't say it surprised me. After all, we'd gotten together the same way, our relationship blooming as her previous one decayed.

———

I was halfway through the second pump of the handshake before I realized what was going on. *Oh, wait, I shouldn't be shaking hands with this person. I hate this person and this is super awkward!*

I pulled my hand away and an uncomfortable silence followed as Ryan and I sized each other up. To break the tension, he turned to a coworker and said, "This is Matteson. We used to do improv together."

Yeah, that's the connection between us, that we did improv together, not that you're FUCKING MY EX-GIRLFRIEND.

Ryan tore our tickets and Sonya and I headed upstairs to the theater. Once we were out of earshot, I told her what had happened.

"I thought he was a friend of yours, you seemed so happy to see him," Sonya said.

"I didn't fully recognize him until after we were already shaking hands."

"Well, the good thing is you look like a total badass now."

She was right. I, the spurned former lover, hadn't cowered when I ran into the new boyfriend. No, I'd greeted him with the smile and handshake of a game-show host. I was a live-and-let-live guy, too happy in life to hate my ex's new dude. Sure, I'd behaved this way because of a faulty memory, but neither Ryan nor Kelly would know, which meant I'd earn a few points in my battle to "win" the breakup. (I was still WAY behind.)

Sonya and I were sipping wine at the refreshment table when my phone buzzed with a text from Kelly: *Ryan told me you're at the show. I was already planning on going and I'm on my way. Just wanted to give you a heads-up.*

"So, you know how that guy was my ex's new boyfriend?" I said to Sonya. "Well, my ex texted. She's going to be here too."

"At least you showed up with a girl, right?"

"Very true."

I'm sure meeting my ex-girlfriend wasn't what Sonya had envisioned for our first date. We'd met online, but not through online dating. I'd heard her as a guest on a podcast and a Google search had revealed her to be as cute as her adorable voice implied. Via Twitter I learned she lived in Chicago, but would be working in Los Angeles for a few months, so I sent her a tweet telling her I loved her on the show and followed up with this: *I see you're going to be in Los Angeles. If you'd like someone to show you around, I'd love to play tour guide.*

I immediately regretted sending the message. Making the offer in a public forum was dumb. If anything happened to Sonya in the next six months, the authorities would search her social media accounts and I'd become a prime suspect. I might as well have sent this message: *I see you're going to be in Los Angeles. If you'd like to spend some time kidnapped and living in a pit I've dug in my basement, I'd love to play your kidnapper. Can't wait to smell you!*

Just as Bridget had surprised me with a yes, so too did Sonya. This asking-girls-out thing wasn't as hard as I thought. Sonya did warn me that her friends and family, and possibly a few mob hit men, knew who I was and where I lived, so there would be retribution if I turned out to be a cannibal. If she'd known she was going to meet my ex-girlfriend on our first date she might have preferred to be made into a lamp shade.

———

A few minutes after the show started I saw Kelly slip into a chair across the room. I pulled the front of my shirt in and out, fanning my chest, trying to battle the heat suddenly churning in my stomach. The feeling of nausea was not dissimilar to the one that occurs at the beginning of a courtship. How poetic of my body to bookend our relationship with queasiness.

During intermission Kelly approached and said hello. She nervously twisted her wineglass as we spoke, which made me happy. I introduced Sonya and the two of them fell into "hey-so-nice-to-meet-you" patter, their voices getting higher and higher as they strove to prove who was the friendliest. Luckily, the break wasn't long, so we didn't have a chance to discuss much more than Murray. Thank God for the dog or we'd have nothing to talk about.

"I decided I don't like her," Sonya said once we were back in our seats.

I decided I liked Sonya.

When the show ended, we headed toward the exit. Kelly was having a conversation across the room so we'd escape without the awkward goodbye. But we couldn't evade Ryan, who stood by the exit holding a garbage bag. I didn't want to talk to him, but at least this was a best-case scenario; it's impossible to feel threatened by a man wearing a name tag and holding a trash receptacle.

"It was great to see you," he said. "Been performing any improv lately?"

My inadvertent friendliness at the beginning of the night had caused him to think we were "cool." But we weren't "cool." While Ryan and I hadn't been close friends, we were at least friendly acquaintances, and you don't move in on the girlfriend of a friendly acquaintance (Section 4.2 of the Geneva Accords). Maybe nothing physical happened between Kelly and Ryan until after we'd broken up, but *something* was going on, and even if there were a dozen other reasons Kelly and I split, what he'd done still wasn't okay with me.

I wanted to say *You knew me, man. You KNEW me. And you did it anyway*. I wanted to see the noxious gas of guilt rise from his belly and putrefy his smile. I wanted to see in his eyes that he understood we weren't "cool." My relationship with Kelly may have started the same way, but at least I didn't think I was "cool" with her ex. *Have a little decorum, Ryan, we're not cool!*

But I didn't say any of that. Instead, I told him about a couple shows I'd done recently and said a polite good night. I wish I took the high road because of a Zen-like compassion for all living things, but really, I just didn't want to make a scene.

I did send a little message as I walked away, though. Get this—I threw my cup in the garbage harder than necessary, hoping some wine would splash on his khakis. It didn't, but still, what a rush!

"Thanks for making me look good in front of my ex," I said to Sonya outside.

"My pleasure," she said. "It was fun to be the hot new piece."

We smiled at each other. The night's drama had made us into a little team, bonding us more than a normal first date would have. I'd kept my cool in front of Sonya, my ex had seen me with a pretty new girl, and I'd been calm and confident in front of the boyfriend. Lots of points scored in my quest to win the breakup, and even if this was purely accidental, they were points nonetheless.

After dropping Sonya off at a large house in the hills above Los Angeles where she was renting a room, I headed home. Instead of cutting over to the freeway, the fastest route, I took Mulholland Drive, the windy vehicular spine of the Hollywood Hills, and enjoyed the warm night with the windows down and my music loud. The lights of LA jumped in and out of view as I navigated the famous curves. Stretched out below me was a city full of women.

I wondered which one I'd date next.

Part II

TURNS OUT I'M GOOD AT DATING

8

THE PEDIATRICIAN
AND THE PODCAST

My experiment was going well: I was meeting women online, dating, gaining confidence, having fun, and keeping all the relationships casual. Then something horrible happened—I met someone I really liked.

I was at a food truck festival in Venice with Kurt and we met up with a group of his friends, which included a beautiful girl named Amber, whom I ended up waiting with in a long line at the grilled cheese truck.

In Los Angeles, having an Instagram account is considered a full-time job, so I was astonished to learn that not only was Amber a pediatrician, she was a partner at her clinic and spent her free weekends going to Tijuana to give treatment to poor children. I consider myself nice—I tip well, give change to the homeless, and donate to Kickstarter projects for one-man shows—but this was another level of philanthropy. Even Mother Teresa was like, *Um, Saturday is kind of me-time....*

After we'd obtained our melted cheese sandwiches for $12 apiece, we sat on a curb eating, talking, and laughing. By the end of the night we were already planning the next group outing, which we both knew was an excuse to see each other again.

Over the next month, Amber and I hung out a few more times, always with a group, and our chemistry was clear. I hesitated to ask her out on a proper date, though, for two reasons:

1. We had mutual friends. A stranger I met online was like a special guest character on *The Matteson Perry Show* who ceased to exist when the episode ended. If it didn't work out with Amber, there would be repercussions, and it almost certainly wouldn't work out since I was in a dating phase known as "trying to make sure it doesn't work out."

2. Amber lived in Orange County. For those not familiar with the Los Angeles area, Orange County is south of the city and is what would happen if The Cheesecake Factory were a county. It is also far away, taking between one and nineteen hours to drive there, depending on traffic.

Despite these reservations, I texted and emailed with Amber almost daily. We had reached the point where I needed to either cut off contact or ask her out. Ending our flirtation would have been the smart move.

I asked her out.

After a very long drive, I picked her up at her condo and took her to dinner. Sexual tension stilted our conversation as we ate. We might have kissed right there in the booth were it not for our overly attentive waiter who popped up every five minutes to see if we wanted to try the house cocktail. *No, we don't, because it looks like Barbicide is the main ingredient in the Blue Sapphire.* Orange County really is the worst.

Back at Amber's condo, we didn't burst into the apartment and shed our clothing, but we did share a shy, slow, polite kiss in her living room. It was nice, the type of kiss exchanged by people who like each other, but are willing to move slowly because they have plenty of time for more in the future.

Which meant it was dishonest, because I didn't want a future with anyone. I was supposed to be living life like I was on a plummeting zeppelin, minutes to live, ripping the clothes off a woman whose name I could barely remember. That was the plan, not this tender intimate stuff. It only took one kiss for me to see Amber and I wanted different things.

I almost had The Talk right then, despite it being only our first date, but she handed me a foil packet filled with homemade chocolate chip cookies and I couldn't say anything. She had me. Snacks are the guy equivalent of flowers. A dozen roses won't register, but a plate of brownies will make us swoon.

———

There was a second date and a third, and though we didn't have sex, our relationship moved quickly. We talked almost every day, sometimes even by phone, this era's "going steady." I needed to have The Talk, but I kept chickening out, wanting to bask in the warmth of her he-might-become-my-boyfriend affection a little longer. After every conversation, like a smoker declaring this to be the last cigarette, I'd vow to bring up our relationship status the next time we spoke.

Then, one night, I got this text: *I think I am listening to a podcast you were on that I shouldn't be.*

I'd done a few podcasts, telling stories or being interviewed, but unless I'd blacked out and gone on *The White Supremacists with STDs Show*, none of my appearances had been offensive or embarrassing. I didn't know what she was talking about.

She explained: *It's the one where you ask for dating advice.*

Shit. I'd forgotten about that. Very shit.

Early on in my dating experiment, before I went out with anyone, I'd gone on my friend's advice podcast and asked how to date casually. Amber was listening to the guy she was dating, who seemed interested in a serious relationship, talk about being not at all interested in a serious relationship.

I had recorded this podcast long before I'd met Amber, so I wasn't being mean or cavalier toward her specifically. Also, we'd only been on three dates, we hadn't had sex, and I'd made no promises of a future together. But it still must have been awful for Amber to listen to me discuss how to hypothetically break it off with a girl, while being said hypothetical girl.

Guess it was time for The Talk. I called her.

"Is what you said on that show true? Is that how you feel?"

I could hear hurt in her voice and felt the urge to fix it. It would be so easy. I could tell her I'd been enjoying casual dating, but meeting her had changed my mind. Her voice would soften as I explained the connection we had, and maybe there'd be tears. She'd ask if she could come over and, fueled by our newfound closeness, we'd have sex for the first time. Telling her what she wanted to hear would have been easy, but I couldn't. Prolonging this any further would be a betrayal of her and my pact with myself.

"Well, I exaggerated my point of view for comedic effect, but, yes, what I said on the podcast is true. I'm trying to stay out of a serious relationship right now."

I told her about my breakup and the vow to be single for a year in an attempt to break my relationship cycle. I explained that though I liked her and wanted to spend more time with her, I couldn't be her boyfriend because I couldn't be anyone's boyfriend. There was only the buzz of cell phone static for thirty seconds. Finally, she spoke.

"I've been single for a while. I'm looking for something real."

———

As I cut into my huevos rancheros with grilled cactus the next Saturday, I told the guys about the breakup. Kurt already knew.

"Yeah, you're not well liked by that group."

This surprised me. The conversation with Amber had been calm and grown-up. In fact, her composure and acceptance had impressed me so much I'd second-guessed my decision. It's a real Catch-22 of relationships that breaking up with someone is one of the best ways to see their true nature.

"Amber's pissed. All the girls are. You're uninvited to Kendra's party next week. And I'm getting a lot of blowback, so thanks for that."

"Sorry. No more dating people I know. I promise. Back to strangers."

We moved on to Evan. Joanna had been in town a few days earlier.

"I didn't see her much. We did meet up at a party of a mutual friend, though. It was going well and I was having a good time, but she asked me to leave because she was feeling weird. I was kind of pissed about it, actually."

"At least you're finally a bit angry with her," Kurt said. I was glad too—this was the first time Evan had been mad at Joanna.

"It did feel good to get mad. But it's pretty much passed. We texted last night. She had a tough day at work and wanted to talk."

Oh, my sweet Evan.

———

I didn't totally believe Kurt when he'd said Amber was angry, but I got confirmation two weeks later in the form of drunken text messages. In Mexico on vacation, and with a few margaritas in her, Amber no longer felt so forgiving. She flicked digital knives at me from south of the border—I was stupid, I'd screwed up something great, and I didn't deserve a girl like her. I did the only thing one can do in such a situation—I agreed with everything she said and apologized.

I'd started my experiment worried about getting women interested in me, but the bigger key to my goal might be staying out of a serious relationship. Not every girl wanted commitment, but some did, so I needed to make my intentions clear early on. I vowed not to slip so close to the event horizon of a relationship again.

9

THE GROUPIE

Kurt, Evan, and I were at Bros' Brunch enjoying pumpkin crepes when I laid out my latest dating predicament. I'd gotten a girl's number, but I was unsure if I should call her, not because of shyness or fear, but because I didn't know if I'd gotten the right girl's number.

I sometimes host a live show called *The Moth,* which features people telling real stories from their lives based on a theme. A couple nights earlier I'd done a show and as I left, a group of three women and one man said, "Great job." I nodded a thank-you and kept walking, but before the end of the block I heard steps behind me and turned to see the guy from the group.

"Hey, I'm Will. My friends and I were about to go have some pie and would love to buy you a slice."

Groupies at a rock show flash their breasts to get backstage so they can blow the lead singer. Storytelling groupies wait patiently outside to buy the performer a slice of pie. I accepted the invitation and we walked back toward the women.

"One of my friends digs you," Will whispered as we approached the trio. Unfortunately, he did not deem it necessary to mention which friend dug me. I was now a romance gumshoe trying to solve what I call The Case of the Mystery Pie.

The setting for this mystery was a Marie Callender's. I ordered my usual, pecan, straight up, no ice cream, and mulled over the three suspects in front of me. None wore a wedding ring. It could be any of them. This was going to be a long night.

Suspect 1—Linda—Approximately five-three, cute, round face, hipster dress, wide smile, architect's apprentice. A sweet girl with an aura of shyness.

Suspect 2—Mary—Approximately five-six, slender build, freckled face, in graduate school for social work. The most attractive of the three women.

Suspect 3—Helen—Approximately five-eight, muscular, dressed in a T-shirt and jeans, long blond hair. Not unattractive, but not my type. Of course, an undying love for me and my comedic stylings could sway me.

An hour later, there was only crust left on the plates and I had no leads. I had hoped someone would say something to incriminate herself or maybe I'd catch sight of a tattoo of my face on someone's arm, but I got no hint at all as to who liked me.

We walked out to the sidewalk to say our goodbyes and no one offered their number, let a hug linger, or asked to get together again. If I hadn't known one of them liked me, I would have gone home happy to have fans buy me pie, but now I was frustrated. I wanted my groupie!

"This was fun," I said. "We should all stay in touch."

I thrust my phone in front of me, where it stayed for a few awkward seconds.

"Uh, yeah, let's trade numbers," Mary said as she reached for my phone. I was most attracted to Mary, but her lack of enthusiasm made me think she might be a patsy.

As I walked to my car I gave my secret admirer one more chance, saying, "I'm easy to find on Facebook! Matteson Perry, with two *t*'s."

———

"I don't know if you're doing this groupie thing right," Evan said when I finished the story.

He was right. I'm guessing the lead singer of Def Leppard never shouted out *I'm easy to find on Facebook—two* p's *in Leppard!*

"I don't know what to do," I said. "It's been two days and I haven't heard from Mary. I could contact her to ask who liked me, but if it was actually Mary, I might ruin it."

"Yeah, I don't think you should text her," Kurt said. "Let the groupie come to you. That's like the number one rule of groupies."

Waiting was the only move.

Finally, almost a week after pie night, I got a break in the case. Mary texted: *It was great to meet you the other night! Thanks for getting pie with us. You should find Linda on Facebook. Her last name is Marshall.*

So it was sweet, quiet Linda. I couldn't blame her for being shy; it can be hard to approach a hero (is *hero* too strong a word? I don't think so). I friended Linda on Facebook and asked her if she'd like to get a drink. She said yes and (I assume) screamed like a girl suffering from Beatlemania.

———

Any usual date nerves were nonexistent because when dealing with a groupie, you just sit back and enjoy the idol worship, right?

Although our interaction probably wouldn't qualify as "worship," the date did go well. My jokes landed, my stories fascinated, and her body language was responsive. I felt like a boxer fighting an opponent who had been paid to take a dive.

Despite the ease, the date did feel a little strange; she knew me so much better than I knew her. Linda had seen several of my stories, either live or on YouTube, so she knew a lot about me already.

Before I'd told her where I grew up she mentioned that she loved Colorado. During a discussion of jobs, I mentioned working in Alaska and she said, "Oh, I like this one," referring to a story I'd told about the experience. She seemed to know the basics of my life, while the only thing I knew about her was that she liked me (an admirable trait, I'll admit). I spent the date trying to shrink the knowledge gap by asking her questions, but it never felt like we were on even footing.

At the end of the night, as we made goodbye-small-talk by Linda's car, I fretted over the hug or kiss question. I'd had a nice time, but I could tell I wasn't passionate about this girl. It felt strange to be only getting to know Linda when she was already certain she liked me. I decided to go with a hug, to take things slow, so I could catch up.

I leaned toward her with my arms in hugging position, but

found her chin pointed up, her eyes closed, and her lips prepared. *Okay, I can give her a little peck good night; that doesn't send any big message.* Before I could pull away, Linda grabbed the back of my head and enveloped me in a full-on makeout session.

When we finished, she asked if I was free Wednesday.

"I'm not sure. . . . I'd have to check my calendar. . . ."

"Okay," she said, staring at me. She wanted me to check right then. I pulled out my phone.

"I guess I'm free."

"Great! My friends and I are going to a beer-tasting concert event. You should come."

I could learn a thing or two from Linda. She'd gotten a make-out session and a second date out of me when I wasn't sure about either—the girl was a closer.

———

When I spotted Linda in the back corner of the brew pub, my stomach dropped—I'd walked right into a trap. Four female friends sat around her like a royal court. I tried to hug Linda hello and she again snuck in a kiss. One of her friends "aahed" while another "oohed." I ordered food, but thirty minutes after my hamburger arrived it remained almost untouched, as I'd been too busy answering questions to eat. This wasn't a social hangout; it was the Silver Lake Inquisition. Her friends were measuring my worthiness for dating Linda. The matter of whether I wanted to date Linda was not taken into consideration.

At the end of the night, I overheard my good reviews as Linda hugged her friends goodbye—*He's great; a keeper; so nice.* It did feel good to pass a test, even one I hadn't wanted to take in the first place. Linda texted me before I got home, telling me what a good time she'd had and how much her friends liked me. Apparently, she wasn't familiar with the dating technique known as "playing hard to get."

It was two weeks before I saw Linda again, a purposeful break to slow things down. I was using a technique called Plotting Points, which I'd learned from Grant (the friend who told me about Burning Man). The idea behind Plotting Points is that it's not the number of dates that signifies the seriousness of a relationship, but the frequency of those dates. Three dates in a week means something different from three dates in a month, despite the number of dates being the same.

How to Plot Points in a Relationship

1. No more than one date per week. At this pace, the relationship can remain casual for a long time.
2. Don't make specific plans for the next date while on the current date.
3. Maintain continuity between dates by keeping in touch via text.
4. When you do set the date, make it a few days or a week in the future, buying further time while confirming interest.

The goal of Plotting Points is to avoid having The Talk for as long as possible. And sometimes, when Plotting Points is executed well enough, the actions have spoken loud enough to render The Talk unnecessary. If you see someone less often than you take your garbage out, it's probably not a very serious relationship.

After being "busy" (playing a new video game) for a couple weeks, I set a date to see a movie with Linda. The time away hadn't dampened her excitement. She spent the whole movie stroking my hand with her thumb, laughter and soft looks punctuated dinner, and at the end of the night she invited me into her apartment.

"I like you," she said, stroking my hair during a break from kissing.

"I like you too." I said it out of instinct, but instantly knew my "like" did not equal her "like."

For guys, the beginning of dating can feel like a series of trials they must pass to earn the approval of the girl. Wouldn't it be nice to avoid all that? With Linda I had. Dating her was like being preapproved for a credit card. No credit check necessary, just start spending.

But in reality, the one-sided nature made me uncomfortable. It felt like my desire to be a couple was irrelevant because she'd already made up her mind. And despite her certainty, I knew she didn't like the "real" me because she didn't know the "real" me. No, she liked the idea of me, the me she'd seen onstage, me at my wittiest and most charming. I'd kept up the performance for three dates, but I couldn't play the role forever.

After my recent experience with Amber, I didn't want to lead someone on again, so I left without having sex, because no matter how well I Plotted Points, Linda wouldn't get the message. I broke it off a few days later. The lack of hate-filled text messages told me I was improving.

I was happy with my progress as a responsible casual dater, but I did have one regret. My first encounter with a "groupie" had ended without my having done the one thing you're supposed to do with a groupie—have sex. I should have at least snorted some cocaine off her breasts in the back of my tour bus. Of course, I'd never done cocaine and didn't have a tour bus. Maybe I could have eaten ice cream off her breasts in the back of my Jetta? That's kind of punk rock, right? Though, the problem there is that ice cream can get pretty messy and it would be a pain for her to clean the stickiness off. *NO, STOP IT, MATTESON! You're being too nice. Cleaning chocolate syrup and peanuts off your breasts is the price you pay for getting close to a STAR!* (Or the host of a nonprofit storytelling show with a small following.)

10

THE SLAYING OF
HIGH-SCHOOL-MATTESON

"I'm going to see Michelle Glimmermen next week," I said as I dug into my waffle with fig syrup.

"Who's Michelle Glimmermen?" Kurt asked.

"Uh, she's only the prettiest girl in school."

I told Evan and Kurt the tale.

―――――

On the first day of Christmas break my senior year of high school, my friends and I planned a party at my friend Pedro's house. Behind his family's main house was an old bunkhouse, a remnant from the property's days as a ranch, which they'd transformed into a sort of rumpus room, with old shag carpet and a mishmash of garage sale furniture. We had spent many nights hanging out there, doing what teenage boys do—playing video games and passing gas.

But this party was going to be different from the average fart-fest. Pedro's little sister, Melanie, who was two grades younger than us, was going to be there with her friends, including Michelle Glimmermen.

Michelle Glimmermen had created a stir when she'd shown up at school in the fall. Beautiful, tall, and athletic, she had the glow of youth but the body of an early-bloomer adult. I thought she was the prettiest girl in school, which meant she might as well be the prettiest girl in the world. Smarts (all honors classes) and a great laugh, deep and loud, rounded out the total package that was Michelle Glimmermen.

Before the girls arrived, there was much jockeying between my friends over who would hook up with whom. The one person I knew for sure wouldn't be getting lucky was me. At that point I'd never kissed a girl, so I had little optimism I'd bone down, boink, take the piggy to the market, do the humpty dance, knock boots, lay pipe, pork, ride the baloney pony, score, or [insert any other horrible term teenage boys use for sex acts].

The party started slow, with the boys and girls segregated, but a suggestion by Pedro that we use the hot tub livened things up. The listed capacity was four, but we fit in ten people, making a warm soup of teenage hormones with slippery legs intertwining under the surface. Boys' legs being as hairless as girls' at that age meant it was often impossible to tell whose leg it was under the bubbles, but it was still exciting.

Because the hot tub was so full, girls were sitting on laps, and Michelle Glimmermen ended up on mine. I thought it must be an accident, that she'd only chosen my lap because no other option was open, but we talked and joked and she never got up, even when a seat was available.

While having the prettiest girl in school sitting on my lap thrilled me, I had a constant worry about getting an erection. It's ironic that men spend the last twenty years of their lives hoping they can get a boner, but the first twenty often praying they won't. There's millions to be made with a reverse Viagra for teenagers: *To be boner-free, take one pill before math class or a school dance. If your nonboner lasts more than four hours, steal the Victoria's Secret catalog from your mom's mail pile.*

If I needed further confirmation of Michelle Glimmermen's interest, it came when we were back inside and she asked if I wanted a massage.

"Sure, but only if you want to," I said, giving her a chance to correct the mistake I assumed had occurred.

"Here, lay your head down in my lap."

As I lay there, the number 73 popped into my head. My friend Ron had often cited studies showing that 73% of massages between men and women resulted in a sexual interaction. This stat was probably bullshit, but because of Ron's confidence and specificity, I believed it. Surely, some university was running a massage-to-hookup experiment and crunching the numbers. And that meant I had a 73% chance of hooking up with Michelle Glimmermen.

Her hands moved in mirrored circles around both sides of my head, her fingernails scratching under my hair. My body tingled from the Jacuzzi, and my feet, positioned close to the fireplace, were toasty. I'd never been so comfy or happy.

Sometime after 2:00 a.m., people settled themselves for sleeping. The choice spots on the couches went fast, leaving only the floor for most of us. Michelle Glimmermen and I ended up next to each other, forced close by the limited space. After lights-out, I could hear the sounds of blankets shuffling and pairs of feet sneaking off to the bathroom. All around me people were getting it on. This was my moment.

But I did nothing.

I could have reached over and rubbed her back or whispered to her or spooned up next to her, but I did none of those things. Instead, every few minutes I'd open one eye and stare longingly. I was terrified she'd catch me, but also hoped I'd find her staring back. I only stopped looking when the sound of her breathing told me she was asleep.

———

"And nothing ever happened with her after that?" Kurt asked.

"We were sort of flirty at school for a couple weeks, but then she made out with this basketball player Jack Coleman."

"Jack Coleman. He sounds like a real dick," Evan said.

Jack Coleman *was* a real dick! Like a high-school movie cliché, I'd lost the girl to the asshole jock. I hated him, but I wasn't angry with Michelle Glimmermen. We weren't a couple, and for all she knew, I was a eunuch.

"And you're seeing this girl when you go home for Christmas?" Kurt asked.

"Yes, I am."

I hadn't kept in touch with Michelle Glimmermen over the years, other than sporadic Facebook interactions, but a month earlier we'd met up at a party when she had visited LA. We'd gotten along well, so I'd asked her if she'd go on a date with me when I was home for the holidays. Though of course I didn't call it a date.

"We should hang out when I'm in town," I'd said.

Translation of the Phrases Guys Use
when Setting Up an "Innocent" Social Interaction

- Let's chill = Let's date

- Wanna hang out? = Wanna date?

- We should get together = We should get together . . . for a date.

- We should grab a drink/bite/snack/meal = We should grab a drink/bite/snack/meal and I will pay for the drink/bite/snack/meal and that will mean we're on a date.

- I was thinking of going to that new play. Would you want to come? = I would never go to a play, but I think it will entice you into a date with me and make you think I'm sophisticated.

- Do you want to go hiking this weekend? = No one except a Sherpa has ever gone hiking except as a date, so we will be on a date.

- Can you help me move this weekend? = Can you help me move this weekend? (It's hard to find people to help you move.)

And so, I was getting a drink (going on a date) with Michelle Glimmermen a few days after I arrived in Colorado.

———

From our cozy booth Michelle Glimmermen and I could see the fat flakes of snow meandering to the already white ground outside. We had been at the bar for more than three hours, but neither of us wanted to face the reality of goodbye and the cold weather.

Of all the women I'd dated since my experiment began, Michelle Glimmermen was my favorite yet. Her laugh was as sublime and generous as it had been in high school and she had the vivid complexion, smoldering eyes, and wide smile I remembered. Even her body looked relatively the same, kept trim by yoga.

In stark contrast to the sweaty interactions of my teen years, the evening was calm and comfortable, thanks to my new dating confidence. Knowing when or how to make a move didn't worry me. I could enjoy our date, certain I'd know what to do when the time came. And I very much hoped the time would come. In some small way, hooking up as an adult would help me to finally erase the cowardice of High-School-Matteson. Though I wasn't angry with Michelle Glimmermen for choosing Jack Coleman over me, I hadn't forgotten the pain it caused me. (Obviously. I mean, I am writing about it in a book.)

On the walk back to her apartment, where I'd parked my car, I offered my arm and she took it. Our conversation dwindled as we enjoyed the tranquillity of a world quieted by fresh snow.

"Would you like to come in?" she asked when we reached her doorstep.

I instantly dropped seventy pounds and the hair in my armpits fell out. I was no longer the thirty-year-old conqueror of online dating, the guy with a fuck buddy and a groupie, but once again the undersized and overwhelmed High-School-Matteson. I clinched my hands inside of my pockets, trying to get "Sure" to pop out of my mouth. I thought I'd gotten over this type of anxiety, but this wasn't just some girl from OkCupid; this was Michelle Glimmermen, the hottest girl in school.

Luckily, she saved me by saying, "I have the latest episode of *Mad Men* on my DVR. We could watch that."

Yes, TV. I was going inside to watch TV. High-School-Matteson could watch TV.

"I love *Mad Men*," I said. "That'd be great."

———

We cuddled up under a blanket, watching the episode. Soon we were kissing and as we made out, High-School-Matteson returned, not as a naysayer, but as an awestruck fan. *Holy shit, Future Matteson, you're making out with Michelle Glimmermen! Take that, Jack Coleman!*

We removed our shirts, but the makeout session didn't progress further, fitting for a hookup with a high-school crush. Afterward we lay next to each other and talked about our almost-fling years earlier. She had indeed liked me, but had been as scared and unsure of the dating process as I.

"When we didn't hook up at the party, I figured you didn't like me like that."

"And then Jack Coleman," I said.

"Yeah. It just kind of happened. He was forward. Not in a creepy way—he just knew what he was doing. No offense."

"None taken." (Some taken.)

"It made it easy. I did feel a little guilty, though. And to this day, he's my dad's least favorite boyfriend, if that makes you feel better." (A little.)

We cuddled and talked for a while longer, but eventually I had to go home. There were holiday responsibilities to tend to the next day, like wrapping presents and making sure I was buzzed enough to deal with my stepmom.

"Well, thanks for living in LA," she said as we got dressed. I could hear in her voice the same regret I was feeling about the unlikelihood this would happen again.

I should have felt triumphant as I drove away—I'd finally made out with Michelle Glimmermen. It wasn't merely a victory for me, but for every shy Nice Guy dumped by a girl for a jock. I was like the Braveheart of awkward teens, though instead of "Freedom!" I would yell "Second Base!"

But I didn't feel like I'd "won." Over the course of the evening she'd stopped being Michelle Glimmermen, the hottest girl in school, and became Michelle, a girl I liked but couldn't date because of circumstance. There was potential between us, like in high school, but it would remain unrealized. That didn't feel like "winning." It felt disappointing.

(Okay, it felt a *little* like winning. I mean, after all, I had made out with THE Michelle Glimmermen. Suck on that, Jack Coleman!)

11

THE "WHAT-IF?" GIRL

Years earlier, before my year of being single, before Kelly . . .

I was living in New York City and had been dating Ann for just over a year. It wasn't going badly, but I could tell it wouldn't last—neither of us had said, "I love you." And a year is a long time to go without saying that to the person you're dating. The more time passed, the more weight the word itself gained. Both of us had started avoiding saying the word *love* at all, in any context. We'd be like, "What a great egg sandwich, I really lo— like it. I liked that egg sandwich. It was very special to me." It's bad form to rank a breakfast sandwich above your partner emotionally.

Since we weren't using the L-word, the cards we exchanged at our one-year anniversary dinner came out sounding like we were signing each other's yearbooks. *It's been great getting to know you this year. Stay cool this summer. XOXO.*

So, things weren't good, but I certainly wasn't going to break up with her, because I was still a Nice Guy at that point, and Nice Guys don't do things that might be emotionally difficult.

One weekend, not long after that awkward anniversary dinner,

Ann and I had plans to attend a concert with my roommate, Dustin, and his girlfriend, Kate Middleton. (When I was writing this book, "Kate" told me she wanted her fake name to be Kate Middleton, so here we are.) At the last minute, Ann had to go out of town for work, so the extra ticket went to Lindsay, a friend of Kate Middleton's.

Being out without Ann excited me. She wasn't against alcohol, but she was a small Asian woman who had no tolerance and therefore rarely drank. And so I drank less. While this was good for me health-wise, I was twenty-six years old and living in one of the greatest cities on Earth; these were not supposed to be my "healthy years." I was excited to go see music, get drunk, and stay out as late as I wanted.

But being out alone wasn't the only reason I was excited. I was also looking forward to spending time with Kate Middleton's friend Lindsay, whom I'd met once before at a party. Nothing had happened between us, except that I'd noticed she had great collarbones. There are breast men and butt men—I am one of the rare collarbone men. We are a small and misunderstood group. Her shoulder blades sprang from narrow shoulders, snaked under the straps of her tank top, and met in the middle, perfectly symmetrical. She had other attractive traits—a beautiful face and nice body—but those collarbones, man!

After the concert the four of us walked to a dimly lit, low-slung bar on the edge of Chinatown decorated with taxidermy animals that stared at us angrily, as if we were the ones who had killed them. It was a random, unknown New York bar, but it was cooler than the coolest bar in my hometown, which made me feel cooler than everyone in my hometown. Which is the whole point of living in New York City.

We hadn't finished our first drink when Dustin and Kate Middleton had to leave because she felt the symptoms of an oncoming flu and wanted to get to bed.

"You guys leaving with us or staying?" Dustin asked.

Lindsay and I peered into our almost empty glasses, then at each other. There was a glimmer of attraction, enough to make us curious. We had the same idea.

"I'd have another, if you're game," I said.

"Yeah, let's have one more."

We hugged our friends goodbye and moved to stools at the bar. Four hours later, Lindsay and I were on the fifth iteration of "one more drink." As the night had worn on, we had moved closer together, until we sat shoulder to shoulder. For a while I'd rested my left arm on her thigh, letting it fall there as though by accident. *Oh, that's your thigh? I thought it was some sort of a fleshy armrest.*

The music was loud so we had to speak directly into each other's ears. I felt her breath on my neck when she spoke, and could smell her hair when I answered. Lindsay's hair smelled WAY better than Ann's. I convinced myself this wasn't a matter of different shampoos but of biochemical compatibility.

Around 3:00 a.m., our conversation paused. This was the moment when we were supposed to kiss. I knew it would pass quickly. Soon Lindsay would take a sip of her drink or fix a piece of her clothing that didn't actually need fixing and the moment would be gone forever. But I didn't want the moment to pass. Every ounce of my emotions and hormones pushed me to kiss her. The lone voice of dissent was my conscience.

"You can't kiss her," my conscience said. "I know the relationship with Ann isn't going well, but she's still your girlfriend. You're a Nice Guy and Nice Guys don't cheat."

My conscience was right. I shouldn't cheat. I couldn't kiss Lindsay.

But then . . .

Don't they say the things you regret the most are the things you DON'T do? Isn't life about embracing the now? Aren't we on this planet to live every moment to the fullest? Ann and I are going to break up in the next month anyway, so what's it matter?

I checked back in with my conscience.

"Those are some really good points," it said.

I kissed Lindsay. She kissed me back.

Our kiss became passionate and we were making out right there at the bar and we didn't care who was watching because we were young and drunk and it was 3:00 a.m. in NEW-YORK-FUCKING-CITY and we were doing something WRONG, but it felt right, so GODDAMN RIGHT! It was the kind of kiss they write songs about, the kind of kiss men go to war over! This was it, this WAS LIFE, and we were DOING IT!

So . . . it was a good kiss. My conscience said nothing more for the rest of the night.

Lindsay and I kept making out until the bartender pulled us apart when the bar closed to give us the check. She came back to my apartment where we kissed more, but didn't have sex.

In the morning, after a couple hours of sleep, we hugged good-bye at my door.

"That was fun," she said.

"It was. I should get your number."

I handed her my phone so she could type it in, knowing this was the final betrayal, a sign I didn't consider this a onetime mistake. I was already looking forward to seeing her again, but as she left, I felt something else underneath the excitement—guilt. I had cheated. I was now a cheater.

To defend myself, I will point out that this was pretty mild cheating. On a scale from one to Arnold-Schwarzenegger's-secret-kid, this was like a three at most. I wasn't married and this wasn't a long, ongoing affair. We didn't even have sex. What had happened between Lindsay and me would be considered, in many European countries, a "friendly hello."

But we weren't in Europe. We were in America. So it was cheating.

Ann and I weren't right for each other, but she didn't deserve the pain of getting cheated on. So I wouldn't tell her. We would break up soon regardless, why burden her with the added suffering? The best course of action was to keep this secret. FOR HER. It would be a burden for me to contain this dark truth, but I'd bravely do it, to protect her feelings. Definitely not to make me look better. No, it was a selfless act ALL FOR HER.

As it turned out, I did not have to "heroically" carry the burden of this secret for long. Because I got caught. Less than twenty-four hours later.

Here's how: I wrote an email to Grant telling him what happened between Lindsay and me. That was mistake number one. If you cheat, don't put the evidence in writing. If you feel the need to tell someone, call them, and even then, you should use a burner cell phone, like you're a drug dealer on *The Wire*.

My second mistake was the subject title I chose. It was, and I quote: *So, I cheated on my girlfriend.* Yep, that's the title I used for an email containing information I wanted to keep secret.

When Grant's response happened to arrive while Ann was using my computer, the subject line made her pretty curious about the contents and she read it. A big fight ensued with lots of yelling, mostly from Ann. There was little I could say in my defense, because it was hard to discredit evidence I'd written. *You're not going to believe that asshole, are you?*

Finally I got an opening when she shouted, "How could you sleep with someone else?"

"We didn't have sex," I said, proud to have something to refute. "We just kissed."

A flawless defense, right? Apparently not.

"That's worse," Ann said. "Kissing is WORSE than sex."

First of all, that's not true. Kissing is not worse than sex. Unless you're Julia Roberts in *Pretty Woman,* kissing ALWAYS ranks below sex. And second of all, it would have been nice to know kissing was worse than sex when I was busy NOT HAVING SEX with Lindsay. At the time I'd thought, *We'd better not have sex, it will make things worse.* Turns out it would have been a real win-win.

I had spent the last couple of months wanting my relationship with Ann to end, but that night I fought to keep it together because I didn't want my cheating to be the reason it ended. When people would ask, "Why did you two break up?" I'd have to say, "Because I cheated," and they'd say, "Oh, I didn't know you were a bad person."

And so I spent several hours persuading Ann to stay with me. Not because I loved her and wanted to be with her, but so I wouldn't be a "bad person." Which, of course, makes me a MUCH WORSE PERSON.

I should have said, "I'm sorry I cheated on you, but I did it because I'm unhappy, and we need to break up." That emotional honesty would have been truly "good." Instead, I spent the night convincing her we shouldn't break up. It worked, but it was, of course, only a temporary fix. Six months later we broke up for good without either of us having said, "I love you." Ironically, we probably stayed together longer because I cheated, our relationship sustained by my guilt.

I tried to get in touch with Lindsay after the breakup, but she'd moved out of the country. I'd lost my chance and she became a "What-If Girl."

Occasionally, over the next few years, Lindsay would pop into my head and I'd think, *What if?* What if we'd had a chance to date properly? What if that night was the lightning strike of love? What if she was "The One"?

And the speculative answer to "What if?" was never a realistic *It probably wouldn't have worked out.* No, the answer to "What if?" was always *We would have fallen in love and moved to Seattle to open an artisanal cheese shop and had adorable children who look great in boat shoes.*

It's rare to get a real answer to "What if?" Life goes on and the question fades away. But that's not what happened with Lindsay. Four years later, in the midst of my single year, Lindsay came back into my life. The Ancient Greeks had the Gods of Olympus to manipulate their fate; we have Facebook. One night she popped up in the "People You May Know" feed and my heart jumped.

I clicked on her profile. Her current place of residence was Los Angeles. That was my current place of residence! I dug deeper—she was not listed as in a relationship and her photos showed no evidence of a boyfriend. My "What-If Girl" was single and lived in the same city as I did. CUPID, YOU SON OF A BITCH, YOU'VE DONE IT AGAIN.

I sent a message. She responded. We went back and forth a few times and she invited me to a concert later in the week. I immediately agreed to the plan, seeing as it had worked out pretty well last time I'd gone to a concert with her. I hoped the band would be good, since we'd most likely be using one of their songs at our wedding ceremony.

Yes, dating Lindsay would mean abandoning my year of being single early, but what could I do, MAGIC was at work. If a magician makes a slice of cake appear out of thin air, you don't say, "Sorry, I'm not really eating carbs right now." No, you eat the magic cake, because you don't screw around with magic. Or free cake.

The first band was onstage when I arrived at the concert venue. I stood on my tiptoes to see over the bobbing heads and spotted Lindsay across the room. She looked great, beautiful and stylish in a leather jacket and tight jeans, rock-and-roll armor for her delicate frame.

She saw me and waved. Our eyes stayed locked as I pushed through the crowd. We hugged. There was something in the embrace. It felt special, comfortable, RIGHT. It was the hug of star-crossed lovers finally reunited. There was no doubt my time as a single man was about to come to a storybook ending.

"This is my girlfriend, Nicole," Lindsay said.

She motioned to her left, revealing a beautiful girl with bright blue eyes and the same petite frame as Lindsay. As I said hello, I tried to figure out what "girlfriend" meant. Girlfriend like *This is my best girlfriend whom I get brunch with* or girlfriend like *I am a lesbian and this is my girlfriend whom I make love to because I am a lesbian?*

When Lindsay slipped her arm around Nicole's back I had my answer. They were a pair of hot, hip, young lesbians, the likes of which I thought only existed in American Apparel ads. The absence of boyfriend indicators on Facebook now made sense, as did the many pictures with very close female friends.

This was a real plot twist considering the last time I'd seen Lindsay there'd been *some* evidence she was attracted to guys. You know, the whole making out with me thing. Sure, I have soft skin and listen to a lot of Katy Perry, but technically I am a man.

Was I the last man she'd kissed? Did I drive her to lesbianism? I knew people didn't "turn" gay, but gay people must have a tipping-point hookup, right? What if I was that person? What if kissing me made Lindsay think, *Oh, this is disgusting. That confirms it. Men are not for me?*

But then again, it could be the opposite. Maybe her experience with me was so incredible, she had thought, *If I cannot have this man, I shall have no man!* I preferred the latter interpretation.

Regardless of what role I played in her realizing she was a lesbian, why did Lindsay invite me to hang out? Why would she want to see some dude she made out with one time years ago? And with her girlfriend? It made no sense.

Wait . . .

WHAT IF I'M HERE FOR A THREESOME?

I'd thought fate had reunited us so I could find True Love, but something more important could be in play—sex with two women at once. The universe works in mysterious, horny ways.

Even as I considered the possibility, I knew I'd fallen prey to a classic naive-straight-boy thought process—*How does their sexuality relate to ME and MY fantasies?* But it was possible, right? They could be bisexual. Lindsay had seemed attracted to me. I spent most of the concert having this conversation in my head:

Rational Matteson: Matteson, lesbians are lesbians because they AREN'T attracted to men. They didn't bring you to have a threesome.
Horny Matteson: BUT MAYBE THEY DID! WE DON'T KNOW! WE KISSED HER THAT ONE TIME.
Rational Matteson: No, that's not why we're here. We don't live in a pornography movie where any social encounter can turn into sex.
Horny Matteson: THEY COULD WANT A PENIS AROUND EVERY NOW AND THEN. IT'S POSSIBLE!

There was no threesome, but it was a nice evening. Lindsay and I still had a good rapport and I liked her girlfriend, whose high energy complemented Lindsay's laid-back nature. Between acts, as the roadies swapped out instruments, we talked about movies and Ryan Gosling came up.

"He's so great," Nicole said. "He may be the only man I'd ever sleep with."

"What a coincidence," I said, "he's also the only man I'd ever sleep with."

Ryan Gosling's beauty transcends sexuality.

The Ryan Gosling talk led to a discussion of the movie *The Notebook*. It's the story of how a young couple survives years apart and innumerable obstacles to be together. It's the ultimate weepy romance. As Lindsay's girlfriend spoke about how much she loved it, Lindsay rolled her eyes. Even in a relationship between two women, someone hates watching chick flicks. I held the same opinion as Lindsay.

But I didn't just dislike *The Notebook*; I hated it. Throughout the movie, Ryan Gosling behaves like a psychopath. He threatens to drop from a Ferris wheel if Rachel McAdams won't go out with him. He writes her a letter every day. He buys and refurbishes a house she mentioned she liked one time. This is all bizarre, unrealistic, creepy behavior, and Ryan Gosling being super attractive is the only reason girls find the movie romantic. If you replace him with Steve Buscemi, *The Notebook* becomes a terrifying thriller.

In the middle of my rant, as I explained to Lindsay and Nicole how no one in real life acts the way people do in romantic movies, I realized I was, at that very moment, acting like I was in a romantic movie. I was at this concert because I'd made out with Lindsay four years earlier and I thought it "meant" something. I believed fate had brought Lindsay and me back together, as if God said, *Hold all my calls until I've reunited Lindsay and Matteson. I'll get to fixing world hunger when I get to it!*

I thought I'd learned my lesson with Kelly, but here I was again, seduced by the Grand Romantic Narrative. At the end of the night, Lindsay didn't come rushing out of the bar after me, didn't chase me down to declare her love, didn't kiss me in the rain. That may be how things happen in movies, but life is not the movies, I was reminded once again. Our ending wasn't epic or amazing. The answer to "What If?" was *You'd become friends and hang out occasionally, but nothing beyond that, because penises aren't for her.*

12

RELATIONSHIPS WITH AN EXPIRATION DATE

Having lived in New York City for four years, I still had a lot of friends there and decided to visit for the Fourth of July. The trip kicked off with a barbecue at my friend Robby's house on an afternoon so humid the only thing to do was sit and drink cold beer, which suited me fine. Though I was happy to see all my old friends, another guest piqued my interest as well, a coworker of Robby's named Simone.

"She's very dedicated to her work," Robby explained, "which is good for her career, but bad for her love life. I told her I have a slutty friend visiting, so she should come to the barbecue. I think she'd be up for having some fun."

"We sluts prefer *monogamously challenged*," I said, "but other than that, I'm on board."

When Simone arrived, Robby stopped just short of miming sex motions as he introduced us. He might have been more excited than either of us for this to happen.

"I'll let you two get *acquainted*," he said as he walked away to tend to the hamburgers.

From a physical point of view, Simone was definitely someone I'd like to "have some fun" with—she had a cute freckle-flecked face, a kind smile, and a nice body. She seemed like a great person too. I mean, I had just met her, so who knows, but I was looking for a vacation sex partner, not vetting someone for the FBI. Our short conversation didn't touch on moon landing conspiracies or the power of crystals—good enough for me!

In the past, if I'd been told a girl was interested in me, I would have screwed it up by engaging in a flirting technique known as the Parasitic Organism. I'd have stayed in her presence all night, ignored my friends, and practically followed her into the bathroom—*I'll be right out here, so just holler if you need any help!*

But now, I was becoming good at dating and could flirt without coming across like a recently released convict. I never hovered around Simone, but made occasional eye contact and chatted whenever we were near each other. By the end of the night, I was pretty sure I could have hooked up with her, but I decided to hold off, because I was exhausted. I was in town for another ten days, and if I played this right I could see Simone a few more times. I gave her a hug goodbye and told her I hoped to see her again before I left New York.

"Couldn't close the deal, eh?" Kate Middleton asked as we rode back to their place in a cab.

"That, my friend, was the slow play. Tomorrow I will follow up and ask her to get a drink and come off as a proper gentleman, rather than a drunken horndog just looking to get laid."

"But you *are* a drunken horndog just looking to get laid," Dustin said.

"Tomorrow I won't be drunk," was the only defense I could offer.

———

In the morning, I got in touch with Simone through Facebook. I had plans in the East Village that night, where she lived, so we agreed to meet for a drink afterward.

I emerged from dinner excited to see her, but with a problem. Simone didn't actually live in the East Village. Technically, she lived south and west of the East Village in NoHo, but probably hadn't said so because no one wants to say they live in NoHo, as it's the wannabe cousin of SoHo.

Manhattan geopolitics aside, a mile lay between Simone and me—far enough to be discouraging, but too short a distance to respectably take a cab. Now, a mile is not far, particularly in New York City—I had a commute that involved over a mile of walking when I lived there—but I lived in Los Angeles now, where a mile is VERY far.

Here is an all-inclusive list of reasons why anyone would walk a mile in LA:

- They've had their license revoked because of a DUI.
- They're doing a walk-a-thon to raise money for Chihuahuas allergic to avocado.
- They're a method actor preparing for a role in an action film called *The Walker*. (Tagline: You've got to walk . . . before you die.)
- They're getting some practice in for the zombie apocalypse.

- They're protesting a new law that adds a 5% tax on frozen yogurt.
- They're a tourist.

For me, walking was like using a fax machine—I'd done it before, but why would I use that arcane technology? Yet, sex was on the line, so I set off.

Within a few blocks I was sweating profusely. Perspiration raced down my forehead and dripped off my nose. My T-shirt was turning from light to dark blue. You'd think I'd just run a marathon. All I needed was a tiny cup of Gatorade and a bib number. The worst situation was going on below the belt, where the humidity had caused a condition known medically as Swamp Ass.

A couple blocks before I reached the bar, I stopped at a drugstore and bought deodorant, baby wipes, and baby powder. Next, I went into a thrift store and purchased a shirt for $7. In a dark corner of a relatively quiet block, I threw away my old shirt, put on the deodorant, wiped down my undercarriage, and sprinkled some baby powder in my undies. I gave myself a sniff. Not bad. I might pull this off, "this" being "not seeming like a sweaty garbage monster." I walked the last few blocks as slowly as possible, willing my body not to sweat any further.

———

"You were all the way up at Fourteenth? That's a long walk on a hot night," Simone said as we hugged hello.

"Ah, I didn't notice. It's fun to be back in New York, walking instead of driving."

We sat at the bar for more than two hours, sipping cocktails and getting to know each other better. She was originally from Minnesota, a sports fan, and one of the few people I'd met in my life who knew as much about *Saturday Night Live* as I did. Her smarts—she'd gone to Ivy League schools for both her undergrad and MBA—blended with her midwestern upbringing, creating an approachable sophistication.

I walked her home, and though it was still warm, a slight breeze cut the heat on the now quiet city streets. Of course, there was the ever-present New York City smell of warm garbage, but that aside, a very romantic scene.

"So, this is my apartment," she said when we reached her building. She turned to face me, readying for a good-night kiss. I'd spent enough time proving I was a gentleman. Time to be bold.

"Well, we should go in there."

"Okay," she said, her eyebrows rising in pleasant surprise.

The tension kept us quiet as the elevator rose to her floor. We walked down the hall without a word. As soon as the door lock clicked, I grabbed her shoulders and kissed her hard, pressing her against the wall. She kissed me back with equal force and we stayed there for five or ten minutes before moving to her bedroom, shedding clothing as we went. The sex was fast, aggressive, and over quickly, leaving us both panting. After a brief break, we had sex again, before finally going to sleep only a couple of hours before Simone had to get up for work.

In the morning, I rode the elevator down with a guy in a sharp suit about my age who was probably headed to a job on Wall Street. I, unshowered and wearing the same rumpled clothes from the night before, was clearly doing the "walk of shame." But, here's the thing—I didn't feel any shame. I was the Boy Toy of a High-Powered New York City Businesswoman! No shame in that at all.

————

Two days later, on the Fourth of July, Simone and I sat jammed together in a round booth with six of my friends. Fireworks were popping above the East River, but we hadn't wanted to leave the air-conditioned bar, figuring it would be more patriotic to keep drinking anyway. Above the table Simone and I talked with the group, but below we were having a private, nonverbal conversation. A roll of the eyes from Kate Middleton let me know we weren't being as discreet as I thought.

Around 2:00 a.m. we left the bar. There was talk of more drinks at another venue, but Simone and I departed. In the last hour the hand flirting had escalated to whispered promises of what we'd do to each other that night. Finally alone in the cab (cabdrivers don't count as people), we started making out before we reached the first stoplight.

As the sun started to snake in between the Manhattan high-rises the next morning, we were still awake, cuddling in bed and taking in the fourteenth-floor view. Instead of staying at Dustin and Kate Middleton's place, where I had an air mattress with a slow leak and an insufficient fan, I was in bed with a naked woman, cocooned in AC. This was the exact scenario I'd hoped for when I'd started The Plan—jetting off to cities around the world to enjoy two of my passions: bedding strange women and central air.

For the first time since I'd started dating casually, the postsex cuddling didn't feel strange. I could fully indulge the affair without worrying about leading Simone on with my wondrous cuddles because I was leaving in a few days. I'd stumbled into the perfect situation—A Relationship with an Expiration Date. We had the good stuff of a relationship (sex, intimacy, fun) without any of the nasty side effects (commitment, serious talks, or gross, disgusting feelings).

———

"So I would rate your penis a one," Simone said.

"Excuse me?"

I was nearly asleep and hoped I'd misheard her. I wouldn't expect penis raves, but a one? Yes, it was ugly and weird-looking, but so are all penises. Compared to a sunset or a Monet painting, yeah, my penis deserves a one, but versus other penises I felt it had a fighting chance.

Simone saw the look of dread on my face and continued.

"No, one's a good score. See, my friend and I have a theory that instead of judging penises on objective size, with bigger being better, it should be about individual fit. So we judge on a scale that only relates to us. So less than one means it's too small for me, over one means it's too big, and a one means it's a perfect fit."

"Okay . . ." I said, still not sure how to take this information.

"It's good! Trust me!" she said.

"Well, thank you, then. Or you're welcome?"

———

Simone and I hung out once more before I left and our last night, like the first two, consisted of drinking and sex. The next morning at breakfast was the first time we were together alone, sober, and not having intercourse. It was slightly awkward. Conversation that flowed easily while we were naked felt stilted in a standard dating scenario. It's weird to make small talk with someone who has ranked your penis.

"Does your offer for me to stay with you when I'm in Los Angeles still stand?"

She had mentioned a trip to visit friends the last time we'd hung out, but I didn't remember telling her she could stay with me. I was pretty sure all I'd said was "we should get together while you're there," but I wasn't going to correct her.

"Of course," I said, deciding I'd worry about what the visit meant when the time came. For now, I had bigger things to think about—Burning Man was only a few weeks away.

It had been ten months since the breakup and eight months since I started dating again. In that time, I'd dated almost twenty different women and slept with five of them. Not exactly Wilt Chamberlain numbers, but for me, a lot. Plus, I'd certainly increase my tally at Burning Man. Maybe I'd have sex with five women that week. Maybe I'd have sex with five women on just the first day!

13

WELCOME HOME?

My Burning Man adventure started in San Francisco, in a store on Haight-Ashbury, where I was shopping for "Playa-wear." Playa-wear is the crazy clothing people wear at Burning Man. (The desert where the event takes place is called the Playa, from the Spanish word for "beach"). Playa-wear usually includes one or all of these things: bright colors, lights, bondage gear, masks, lingerie, and thrift store clothes that used to belong to that art teacher you were pretty sure smoked a lot of pot. Basically, you dress like a five-year-old whose parents let him dress himself.

I was shopping with a friend of Grant's named Logan, who was going to ride in to Burning Man with me. So far, my big purchase had been a leather bracelet. It was far from extravagant, something you'd see on the wrist of your average farmers' market vendor, but as I never wore jewelry, it seemed PRETTY WILD. In fact, when I wore the bracelet out of the store, I immediately felt self-conscious and took it off. No need to start the radical-self-expression just yet.

If a leather bracelet felt out there, I certainly wouldn't buy anything from the second store we visited, which looked like the closet of a sex clown. All the clothes were kitsch, tight, and from the "electric" section of the color wheel. I was flipping through a rack of pants, when a salesgirl wearing yellow bell-bottoms and a neon-orange tube top (standard retail uniform) asked me if I needed help.

"Just looking," I said.

"I'm guessing you're going to Burning Man. Are you set for sparkle pants?"

She said this as if sparkle pants were a human essential, like water.

"I would say I'm not well set in the sparkle pants department."

She asked my size, grabbed six pairs of pants, each a different color and pattern, and took me by the hand to the back.

"It's a coed changing room. Do you mind?"

"Uh, that's fine."

Burning Man had begun.

She opened the curtain to reveal an area fifteen feet square occupied by a topless woman and two huge Irishmen in their underwear. While I tried on the different pairs of pants, the salesgirl kept popping her head in and saying things like *Damn, your ass looks amazing in that pair* or *You're going to get so laid in those.* She was good at her job is what I'm saying.

Eventually, I settled on a pair of skintight marine-blue pants worthy of an Olympic figure skater.

"Great choice," she said. "Would you be interested in purchasing a matching bow tie?"

HELL YES, I would be interested in purchasing a matching bow tie.

———

The next day Logan and I rose before the sun to head into the desert. On the way we picked up Logan's friend Alenka, though I wasn't sure we had enough room for another person and their belongings. The trunk was almost full and we still needed to pick up food, water (seven gallons per person recommended), and booze (seven gallons per person recommended).

"Think it will all fit?" Alenka asked. Born in Estonia, raised partially in the United States, and now living in France, Alenka spoke with a subtle, strange, and cute accent. She had angular Eastern European facial features and a fit body, evident despite the hoodie she wore. Sitting on the sidewalk was a growing pile of her stuff. I didn't see how I would make it work.

"I'll make it work," I said. Incredible what you can accomplish when an attractive woman asks.

We stopped in Reno for groceries and found Whole Foods full of Burners pushing shopping carts filled to the brim and shouting advice back and forth. The amount of dreadlocks, tattoos, and "free spirits" was high, even for Whole Foods. I thought our next stop, Walmart, would be less popular with Burners, given the mythos, but it was even more crowded, every register four carts deep. Spending a week without commerce requires a lot of commerce. Our supply cache secured, we departed civilization.

Burning Man is located approximately a hundred miles from Reno. The first twenty miles were an easy drive on the interstate. The remaining eighty miles, spent in a bumper-to-bumper line on a small country road, would take seven hours.

We crawled along, rarely exceeding fifteen miles per hour, sometimes coming to a standstill. Logan and I talked a lot. Alenka alternated between sleeping and bouts of rapid-fire questions on a wide variety of topics: *Where are you from? Are there showers at Burning Man? What do you think about death? What's Brooklyn like? How much art is at Burning Man? Who is Quentin Tarantino?* She was kind of like the hot foreign exchange student I'd hoped would show up in high school.

We passed by a small town, part of an Indian reservation, a blip of civilization amid swaths of barren land. Every home and storefront was dedicated to servicing Burners. Hand-painted signs advertised camping supplies, Playa-wear, bikes for rent. One notice promoted the services of "The only lawyer within 100 miles." The majority of the population's income probably came during the week of Burning Man, for better or worse.

Strangers that morning, by midnight Logan, Alenka, and I were like roommates, riffing on inside jokes and making fun of each other. The sky had darkened completely and a snake of red lights stretched out before us into the darkness. Our energy ebbed and flowed as we tried to manage the purgatory in which we were stuck, at Burning Man, but not yet at Burning Man.

As we inched along toward our destination, some of my excitement turned into nervousness about the week ahead and one aspect in particular—the drugs. Many people attend Burning Man and stay sober the entire time, but drugs are common there.

I'd only done a drug "harder" than pot once in my life and it had come a couple months earlier at a Phish concert while I was in New York. I was not a fan of the band, but Grant had an extra ticket and I thought it might be a good opportunity to try some drugging. A few minutes before the band took the stage, Grant dropped a half-dozen shrooms into my hands. The gray shriveled fungi, each about two inches long, looked like something you'd find while cleaning out a nasty fridge.

"Is this one dose?" I asked. *Dose.* Look at me, using drug slang!

Grant nodded. I looked at the pile of mushrooms again. It looked like more than one dose to me. Shouldn't one mushroom equal one dose? Pouring them into your hand like trail mix didn't seem like a good form of measurement, but I shoved them into my mouth anyway. They tasted horrible, the kind of flavor that makes your body say to your brain, *We are eating poison. I'm going to keep chewing and swallowing, as you command, but just so you know, this is poison.*

After worrying for the first hour that I might throw up, I was able to relax into the sensation. My body tingled, the light show mesmerized, and the music sent my mind pleasantly drifting. I decided I liked doing tripping. It was fun!

So, my first and only experiment with drugs was a positive one (other than getting me to like Phish), but I was still nervous about what was to come at Burning Man. I'd always been anxious around drugs. This is because the DARE (Drug Abuse Resistance Education) program in elementary school had REALLY worked on me, convincing me drugs weren't just unhealthy or dangerous, but inherently wrong and evil. As a ten-year-old I'd vowed to "Just Say No" to drugs and, if need be, happily step up as a snitch. I was a proud American, eager to help George Bush Sr. win the war on drugs.

In college, as drinking and pot use became ubiquitous, my attitude mellowed. Maybe the roots of the marijuana plant didn't reach all the way to hell. But I still didn't partake in drugs, other than very occasional pot use, and even being around them was rare.

But my year of being single meant trying new things, so I wanted to experiment with drugs at Burning Man. I worried my inexperience would make me look foolish, though. What if I snorted some cocaine and everyone stared at me like *Don't you know you're supposed to put that kind of cocaine in your butt?* And then I'd be the dipshit who couldn't tell the difference between regular cocaine and butt-cocaine.

Knowing Grant would be there calmed my nerves a little. After our successful trial at the Phish show, he'd agreed to be my Drug Spirit Guide. I told him that whatever he got, to get some for me too, and tell me how to use it. With Grant's guidance I would get through it, I could do it, I could be a drugger.

———

Around 1:00 a.m., we turned off of the road and onto the dry, silty lake bed, the "Playa." We were close, but our progress remained slow. During another stop, a woman jumped out of the RV behind us, removed her shirt, and started dancing topless in front of the headlights. She spun and gyrated, the long scarf in her hand trailing behind her and contorting in the wind. People honked their horns in support and others joined the woman in celebration.

"Is it time for beer yet?" Alenka asked.

Alenka had wanted a beer for several hours, but I, a Goody Two-shoes even at Burning Man, had asked her to wait. According to the internet, local law enforcement was quick to hand out open container tickets to Burners who started the party too early.

We were still driving, but if I'd learned anything from beer commercials, it was that a woman dancing topless in the headlights of a vehicle means it's time for beer. Logan retrieved a large bottle from the trunk, popped the top, and we toasted our (almost) arrival. A half hour later we were at the entrance.

Normally, at the front gates, the Welcome Committee beckons people from their cars, gives them a hug, and says, "Welcome home." This is a common greeting at Burning Man. Like "aloha" in Hawaii, people use it for hello, goodbye, and several things in between. After the greeting, Burning Man virgins ring a special bell and make a "Playa angel" in the dust.

We did not get this typical spirited welcome. A powerful dust storm rendered our greeter unenthusiastic. The ambassador handed us information guides and pointed us in the direction of our camp.

In the distance we could see lights, but around us, on the farthest road from the center of Black Rock City, there was only darkness. Few of the RVs, tents, and scaffolding structures were lit up. People in goggles and face masks would emerge from the dust storm, leaning against the wind, visible for only a moment before evaporating in the white. It felt postapocalyptic.

We pulled up to our camp and found it empty and dark. No Playa angels, no ringing of the bell, no one at camp to receive us. The energy welling up inside of me, ready to burst forth, had nowhere to go. It was like I'd shot a gun, but instead of a bullet coming out, there was a "Bang" flag.

Twenty minutes later we saw a group of people decked out in various neon colors, blinking lights, and fur coats walking up the road toward our camp. We got out of the car to see if we knew them. A tall man wearing a bloodred top hat and a matching fur vest came running at me. It wasn't until he'd wrapped me up in a hug that I realized it was Grant.

"Welcome home!" he shouted.

The rest of the group surrounded Logan, Alenka, and I, and assaulted us with hugs and names. Now I was excited! I tore through my suitcase searching for my blue sparkle pants and changed into them right there. Grant handed me a beer and a pill.

"It's molly," he said.

"What's molly?"

"It's like ecstasy. Just take it."

I nodded and obeyed my Drug Spirit Guide, popping the pill into my mouth and washing it down with a slug of beer. Guess we were getting this thing cranked right up.

———

I headed out toward the Playa with Grant and a few others. The dust storm had settled, making the lights visible and distinct. They came in every color, most of them blinking, spinning, or moving, all attached to something, either a human, a sculpture, or a Mutant Vehicle, the modified cars that crawl all over the Playa, part transportation, part mobile art piece.

We walked over to what looked like a Chinese pagoda. The structure, the size of a large barn, was powerful and foreboding on the flat desert landscape, but up close the intricate woodwork looked like lace. This was the Temple, the spiritual center of Burning Man and the last thing to burn at the end of the week. Still incomplete, yellow tape cordoned it off so a construction crew could work through the night to finish a structure that would burn to the ground six days later.

In the distance, in the middle of it all, stood the Man himself, a giant neon effigy reaching toward the heavens. I got a little choked up when I caught sight of it. A year earlier, I'd been dumped and depressed, hearing about Grant's awesome trip, and now I was here, experiencing it for myself.

A couple hours later we returned to camp and I joined some people having beers. The jovial group was laughing, hugging, and singing, but I didn't feel a part of it. I stood at the edge of the party, watching quietly, my excitement turning to anxiousness. I didn't know anyone but Grant, and everyone else seemed to be lifelong friends. Not to mention, they were all so at ease with the strange clothes, the partying, the nudity, the drugs.

I felt like a kid on his first night at sleepaway camp—excited about what was to come, but also homesick and worried about making friends. What if the drugs and the people and the weirdness were too much for me? Maybe I was too square for Burning Man. My last thought before falling asleep that night was *I don't know if this is for me. I hope I can last seven days out here in the desert with these people.*

14

ACID MONDAY

Some of my campmates had a tradition known as Acid Monday. How Acid Monday works is that on Monday night you take acid. It's a simple tradition, as the best ones are.

As I spent that day exploring Black Rock City, a pit of nervousness cratered my stomach. I thought about what it would be like to take LSD. I didn't want to freak out during some crazy hallucination and look like an idiot in front of these varsity-level drug users.

After dinner Grant handed me an orange Sour Patch Kid dosed with one drop of liquid LSD and I placed it on my tongue like it was a psychedelic communion wafer. Alenka, sitting across the table from me, rolled her Sour Patch Kid back and forth in the palm of her hand, wondering if she should take it. She had never even tried pot.

"I don't know about this," she said. "Maybe I shouldn't do it. I'm tired anyway. I might just go to bed early."

She glanced up at me, silently asking for my opinion.

"I think you should take it," I said. "I've never done it before, either. We'll stick together and keep each other safe and I bet it'll be a great night. And we'll be able to leave Burning Man without any regrets."

I was pumping myself up as much as her. She popped the candy into her mouth.

"Let's go tripping," she said.

Yes, let's.

After about twenty minutes my hands and scalp began to tingle. Then, my whole body felt alert and adrenal. I asked Alenka how she was doing.

"I don't feel anything. Maybe mine didn't work."

As we all left camp, toward the beckoning lights of the Playa, I felt like a part of the group for the first time, bonded to it by our shared high. Whatever happened on my first acid trip, we were in it together, a platoon of psychedelic explorers marching toward our destiny.

For the first thirty minutes, I silently marveled at the scene around me. On LSD the Playa was even brighter and louder, as if the knob for the world's master volume had been cranked all the way up.

We walked over to the Man. The base was a large three-story building, with a series of arched balconies. On top, the Man stretched up into the sky another fifty feet, a skeletal structure lined with orange neon lights, slowly rotating.

I wandered inside the base structure and climbed the stairs to a window on the third floor, just beneath the Man's feet. Stretched out before me was a vast expanse of blackness broken up by lights. I felt like an astronaut gazing out at the stars from beyond Earth. It was beautiful, moving, and a little bit scary.

I headed back outside and found our group was breaking off in different directions. Some had already walked over to the Temple, while others, including Grant, were about to head to a party. I hesitated, not wanting to get separated from my Drug Spirit Guide, but also being curious to see the interior of the Temple at night while on acid.

"I think I'm going to go catch up with the others at the Temple," I told Grant.

He gave me a hug and said, "Have fun." As I walked away, he watched like a parent dropping his kid off at college, happy to see me heading out on my own, but a little worried about what would become of me.

As I approached the Temple, it occurred to me that the LSD and the craziness of Burning Man might make it hard to find my campmates. I could end up alone, with no Drug Spirit Guide AND no friends.

Normally, getting separated from my group at a party would have threatened to ruin my night, but I felt at peace wandering alone. I didn't need a party, because there was one happening in my body. If I didn't find my group I could spend the night exploring Burning Man and my inner psyche. It would actually be good for me. I could reach enlightenment. Or, better yet, meet a girl.

"Matteson!" someone called.

Oh thank God, a person I know, I don't have to be alone.

I turned to see Brian, a lanky Canadian from my camp. He was sucking on a cigarette and wearing a mangy old fur coat and blue leggings. Classic Burning Man look.

"Where's everyone else?" I asked.

He nodded toward the Temple.

"Yeah. It's not good in there," he said.

"Why not?"

"You'll see."

I left him standing about twenty yards outside the entrance, the closest to the Temple he could smoke. They didn't want someone to accidentally burn it down before they purposefully burned it down.

———

In movies and TV, people on acid experience hallucinations replete with Day-Glo dragons, flowers, and rainbows. I did not experience this. For me, the LSD visuals were only slight alterations. Lights left a trail; patterns shifted and moved; shadows seemed to be alive for a split second. That was really it. But, while I didn't have a conversation with Abraham Lincoln's ghost, some of the things I saw on LSD did trip me out. The Temple tripped me out.

The intricate woodwork, illuminated by bright lights, twitched to life. Every surface quivered, like it was turning from solid to liquid. People packed the central chamber and it felt like I could hear every word, every laugh, every breath. The building, the sounds, the light, and the people were all in sync, pulsating, as if powered by some heart deep underneath the Earth.

I walked back to Brian.

"Yeah, it's not good in there."

We waited for the others to emerge, but after thirty minutes it was time for a rescue. We spotted a few of them in the middle of the Temple, lying on their backs, staring up at the ceiling.

We tried to rouse them, but no matter how much we explained why it "wasn't good" in there, they wouldn't get up. For a moment I had Alenka's attention as she stared deep into my eyes, past my corneas, and into my soul. I readied for her to say something incredibly insightful.

"I think the drug is working," Alenka said.

Guess so.

Brian and I took a seat beside Alenka and Puffin, a Brit from our camp, so nicknamed because his body type resembled that of the barrel-chested bird. For some reason, Brian and I, high on acid, began to talk about Nicolas Cage. Puffin sprang upright, shaken from his trance. He spoke with an accent as proper as the queen's.

"Is someone speaking of Nic Cage in the Temple?"

"Yes," I replied.

I was embarrassed, but Puffin nodded as if I'd just said something very wise. He approved of my nontraditional spirit animal.

———

A group of us exited the Temple and started walking with no particular destination in mind. Beyond the periphery of the Temple we slipped into the darkness of the desert, giving my sensory perceptors a break. Getting away from the sound and light felt good, like diving into a cool lake on a hot day.

The flatness of the land made it hard to determine distance. Only when I'd look back and see how small the Temple had become could I be sure we were moving at all. We came to an art installation that looked like a giant Slinky made of neon and all lay underneath it, mesmerized by the lights spinning above us.

Next, we climbed aboard a life-sized pirate ship, made to look like it had shipwrecked in the desert. We then came across an art car shaped like a giant metallic octopus with arms moving up and down and spewing fire. A glowing mushroom blasting techno music drove by us, trailed by three motorized cupcakes. We stayed as quiet as we could in a "meditation egg," eventually running out in a fit of giggles. Inside a mirror maze we scared each other over and over again. We drank from the breasts of a minotaur and found not milk but a White Russian cocktail.

All my life, I hadn't understood why people did drugs, but that night I unraveled the mystery: it's because drugs are really fun! I laughed and laughed, often until I cried, gasping for air, and clutching my stomach. Everything I encountered felt new, not just to me, but to existence, as if it had just been invented.

The LSD had an emotional component as well. I was bonding with these six people. By the end of the night, we didn't feel like six individuals but rather, like six pieces of a whole. If one of us had to go to the bathroom, well, then, we all had to go to the bathroom, and we'd march off to find the nearest latrine together. This bond wasn't temporary; I'd feel most comfortable around these people for the rest of the week.

Eventually we returned to camp and had a joyous reunion with the others.

"Where have you guys been?" Grant asked.

"I don't know," I replied. "Walking around."

"You were gone for five hours."

"Huh," was all I could say.

———

As I got ready for bed, I thought about how much had changed in twenty-four hours. The day before I'd been nervous about taking drugs and unsure if I should even be at Burning Man. Now I had six new best friends and I loved LSD. Oh, and also, I understood the Beatles song "Lucy in the Sky with Diamonds." "Kaleidoscope eyes." I get you, John and Paul, I get you. Because I'm a drugger now.

15

YOU CAN ONLY UNDERSTAND BURNING MAN IF YOU'VE BEEN THERE (BUT I'LL TELL YOU ABOUT IT ANYWAY)

The mornings at Burning Man all started the same, with me waking up and thinking, *I don't know if I can keep doing this for the rest of the week.* I was having a blast, but the extreme environment was taking a toll on me. No matter how late I went to bed, the heat made it impossible to sleep past 10:00 a.m., so I was always exhausted when I awoke. I'd stumble from the yurt and make the five-minute walk to the latrines dressed only in boxers. Wearing nothing but underwear in public would normally mortify me, but the topless women and naked old men rendered me an unnoticed prude.

Nudity aside, Black Rock City felt like a tranquil community in the mornings. People sat in front of their camps having coffee, others transported supplies in wagons, and someone was always building something. It was practically Amish, though instead of barns, people were raising peyote dens. This sense of community, and my friends in camp, would enliven me and before long I'd forget how tired, hot, and sore I was.

Every afternoon my camp threw a five-hour festivity with music and free booze. These parties were what we gave to the Burning Man community, our contribution to the gifting economy.

There is (almost) no commerce at Burning Man—no snack stands, no T-shirt vendors, no supply stores. No one is allowed to sell anything. The only things one can buy at Burning Man are ice and coffee. The ice, because it would be too hard to keep food fresh without it, and the coffee to raise money for the nearby community, as a thank-you/sorry.

The idea behind the commerce ban is to encourage self-sufficiency and generosity. Some mistake this for a bartering system, but gifting is different. It's not "I'll trade you some batteries for some duct tape." Gifting means contributing to the community in the good faith that what you need/want will be provided by others. There are food camps, party camps, spa camps, bar camps, game camps, nap camps, etc. Whatever you might need, chances are a camp is providing it for free. Our camp provided one of the essentials—ice-cold daiquiris.

While bartending at one of our parties a friend introduced me to another new drug: cocaine. He started to hand me the bag, but I waved my hand.

"No, I don't know how to do it. Just make me one. Make me a cocaine."

He scooped up a little pile of white powder with the tip of a key and held it under my nostril. I sniffed, felt a tingle in my sinus, and a medicinal taste in the back of my throat.

You know how in movies people on cocaine talk about how great they feel? It's because cocaine makes you feel really great! I felt like I'd woken up from the best night of sleep in my life, on a bed made of clouds, next to a supermodel heiress to a diamond fortune. I shook cocktails and met people and danced and laughed and oh my God I was SO good at this—I WAS THE GREATEST BARTENDER WHO EVER LIVED. What was all this nonsense about cocaine being a drug? It was more like a health elixir or Flintstones snortable vitamins.

I could see how something that made me feel this good could become a problem, so I promised myself I wouldn't do any back home. It would be easy for cocaine to worm its way into everyday life.

- *Oh, going to the club will be so much more fun on coke. It's the weekend. No big deal.*
- *Oh, going to the bar will be so much more fun on coke. Thursday's practically the weekend. No big deal.*
- *Oh, going to the grocery store will be so much more fun on coke. It's Monday, but every day's a weekend when you're on coke. No big deal.*

On days when I wasn't bartending I'd go explore. The expeditions would start with a specific destination in mind, a performance or a party or a food camp, but I rarely reached my intended target. There were too many distractions along the way.

Oh, there's a giant teeter-totter that sends riders twenty feet in the air. Better ride it. And here's a guy carrying a tray full of pancakes while wearing nothing but a syrup holster. I could eat a couple pancakes. What's that in the distance? A man zooming across the desert, surfing the sand on a skateboard, pulled by a large kite. I should watch that for a while. And hell no, I'm not going to walk past this roller disco rink without taking a spin.

The people, and their nudity, were spellbinding too. Though it wasn't the many topless women who stick most in my mind, but rather, a penis. A large penis. The largest I'd ever seen. At least ten inches long, flaccid, and as thick as a French baguette. Had I seen this penis in a movie I would have assumed it was CGI, but here it was, in the flesh (oh, so much flesh).

I casually stood near the man getting as many glimpses as I could. That what I had and what he had both went by the name *penis* seemed like a scientific fallacy. A house cat and a lion may both technically be felines, but you can only adopt one of them at the local pet fair. I couldn't imagine there was a woman in the world for whom this penis would be a "one."

I forwent full nudity, not only because of shyness, but for comfort and safety reasons too. A lot of men at Burning Man were way too cavalier with their wangs for my taste. On construction sites in the real world people wear helmets and steel-toed boots, but here I saw a guy pounding nails without so much as a jock strap. And what about penis sunburn? My penis had seen less direct sunlight than a vampire and I wasn't going to risk him turning to dust.

Not all my wanderings were dedicated to schlong gazing. When I returned to the Temple in daylight I could see the walls were covered with photos of departed loved ones, messages scrawled on the wood, and little tchotchkes of significance. At the end of the week, these things would burn with the Temple, providing psychic release for the person who had placed them.

A Nerf football served as the conch as people took turns sharing stories of loss, heartbreak, and death. When they'd finish, usually in tears, there'd be cheers of support, applause, and group hugs.

It felt like a combination AA meeting–funeral—so, you know, not so fun. And I was at Burning Man for fun. But I stayed for a while anyway. Despite my initial apprehension, I listened intently as people talked about suffering and loss and the healing nature of being "home." I didn't laugh or make snarky comments, even when a man went on and on about the death of his pet snake, Mr. Slithers. The pain and openness in some of the stories moved me to tears. Instead of getting drunk and watching topless girls gyrate, I was here, taking some spiritual medicine, and feeling better for it.

(This was my only trip to the Temple—the rest of the week I chose the gyrating girls.)

———

Between the drugs, parties, and new friends, Burning Man was living up to all my expectations. Except in one important way: I was not having sex. Before Burning Man I assumed it would go something like this:

Burning Man Official: Welcome to Burning Man. Just a couple questions for you. Did you bring your penis?
Me: Yes, I did.
BMO: Perfect. Head that way and you'll see a pile of naked, horny hippie-chicks all waiting to be sexed.
Me: Just a heap of women waiting to have sex with me like some sort of fuck-pile?
BMO: Exactly. A fuck-pile. You can't miss it.

But there was no fuck-pile. No orgies. No sex at all.

The problem was that sexual encounters at Burning Man were always now-or-never scenarios. Without cell phone reception or internet, there was no meeting up later. Over the past year I'd become good at getting numbers and asking women out online, at setting up dates, but I hadn't pulled off any one-night stands. At Burning Man they all had to be one-night stands and the feat was even harder because I'd have to convince a girl to have sex with me on an air mattress covered in sand in a yurt I was sharing with three other dudes.

I came close to having sex a few times, but it never worked out. I danced with one woman for an hour before she introduced me to her husband (great guy). Another woman licked my nipple after I served her a daiquiri, but this was just Burning Man's version of a tip. A beautiful young woman had me drink from a large golden goblet and asked me to frolic with her, but completely forgot who I was within ten steps' worth of frolicking.

About five days in I finally managed a kiss, but after twenty minutes of making out, my partner needed to tell me something.

"I came to Burning Man with my boyfriend."

"Oh, do you guys have an open relationship?"

"I don't think so."

I figured I could round *I don't think so* up to *NO*.

"Have you been together a long time?"

"Yeah, seven years. We live together."

Instead of returning to kissing, we talked about her relationship. Thanks to my emotional support and insight, she stopped making out with me and went to find her boyfriend.

Despite these whiffs, I wasn't worried, because I had a backup plan. There was a camp that threw orgies (in an air-conditioned dome) as their "gift" to Burning Man. At the Orgy Dome, I figured, I could finally let my eroticism run wild and have sex wearing nothing but a wolf mask, both literally and metaphorically.

But even there I ran into a problem—single men were not welcome at orgies. Which, of course, makes sense. If orgies allowed single dudes, orgies would be nothing but a bunch of single dudes oiling each other up and saying, "So when's this orgy kicking off? Where the ladies at?"

With my last resort a failure, I had to accept the depressing truth—I couldn't get laid at Burning Man. Surprisingly, I was okay with this, because something more important than sex happened to me: I fell in love.

With a man.

No, I didn't come out of the closet or discover I was bisexual. What happened to me was much gayer than that—I fell head over heels in friendship with Brian.

From Acid Monday on, Brian and I did just about everything together. We ate together. We took bartending shifts together. At night we stood side by side as we wandered from art piece to art piece and party to party. Often we'd share one beer, passing it back and forth between sips. By Wednesday we were calling each other "hubby." *Need some more coffee, hubby? Where should we go tonight, hubby?* Some people started calling us the cutest couple in camp. I've had several good male friends in my life, but I'd never fallen this fast before.

Our relationship came to a head on Saturday night, the end of the week, when the entire population of Black Rock City (56,000 that year) formed a giant ring of madness around the Man to watch it burn. The fire started small, but grew rapidly, eating up the wooden support structure and crawling up his legs. Pockets of explosives created inferno blasts, the heat of which we could feel on our faces two hundred yards away.

Though flames engulfed the entire structure, it took over an hour to fall, another example of the tension-and-release pattern that epitomizes the Burning Man experience. The yearlong buildup, the painstaking drive in, even the EDM music—with its building verses and climactic bass drops—is geared around this dynamic. When the Man finally toppled, chaos erupted. People sang and yelled and ran and cried and stripped and kissed and prayed and danced. I threw my coat to the ground and joined a crowd stampeding around the ashes, howling up to the heavens. (I should mention I was on LSD again.)

When cogent thought returned, I was panting and covered in sweat like a werewolf who had returned to human form. Shoeless and shirtless, wearing only my blue sparkle pants and a matching bow tie, I couldn't help but laugh. *Matteson Perry from Fort Collins, Colorado, how in the hell did you end up in the middle of the desert, dressed like a freak, and tripping on acid?* It wasn't a feeling of guilt, but one of excitement and pride. I had really done this thing.

I spotted Brian through the smoke. I had to tell him how I felt. I ran to my hubby.

"Brian, before the drugs wear off, I need to tell you that I love you."

I'd never told a man, other than my father, that I loved him before. I'd loved male friends, but I hadn't ever said it out loud in total sincerity like this. I grew up in the sort of macho Middle-

America culture where you don't express emotions so boldly. It wasn't cool to lean over during a football game to say, "That touchdown was almost as special as you are, bro!"

But it felt good to say it, right to say it, a step away from the fear I'd always had of losing control, of being vulnerable.

Brian choked out, "I love you too," through his tears. Hubby's a bit of a crier.

Not long after, I persuaded Alenka and Brian to climb a large structure made out of a cargo net to watch the sunrise. As we sat shoulder to shoulder in the giant hammock, an Australian girl asked if we wanted some chocolate with mushrooms in it. It was 6:30 in the morning and we'd been up all night on drugs. We didn't need anymore. Nonetheless, we each took a piece of the psychedelic candy bar. Some people believe drugs are like laundry and shouldn't be mixed. Those people are boring. Though their whites are probably whiter.

"I swear there was a word I knew before I came to Burning Man," I said. "It had two letters and meant the opposite of 'yes.'"

"I haven't the foggiest," Brian said.

A few art cars were still crawling around the Playa. Mountains, invisible at night, leapt into place, suddenly vivid and towering over the landscape. The almost full moon hung in the sky. We watched in silence, the mushrooms enhancing the spectacle, as the sun slipped upward, seeming to gather speed as it went.

Though the sex and dating of the past year had been fun, I'd missed the closeness and connection that comes with a relationship, but I felt like I'd gotten it at Burning Man, outside the realm

of romance. For the first time I truly believed I didn't NEED a relationship. I'd come to Burning Man looking for sex, but ended up
learning of its limits.

And if all this sounds like dumb spiritual hippie nonsense, well,
I'm not surprised, because you haven't been there, maaaaaaaan, so
you don't GET Burning Man.

(Sorry.)

16

THE GOLDEN GIRL

"If your tent is too hot for sleeping," I said to Alenka, "you can join me in my yurt if you like."

Though I'm sure her tent really was hot, my offer was not altruistic. This was my desperate last attempt to have sex at Burning Man. I know I just talked all about my spiritual evolution and how I didn't need sex for my experience to be complete, but, come on. SEX.

Alenka stared at me for a moment, aware of the subtext. Our relationship had been platonic all week, but as we'd watched the sunrise she'd rested her head on my shoulder and I'd thought something had shifted. But she was hesitating. Maybe I was wrong. Finally she spoke.

"Okay, sounds good."

We crept into the yurt, careful not to wake up my roommates. Alenka shed her coat and revealed her golden body. And I don't mean "golden body" as a metaphor. Her body was literally painted gold. Alenka had dressed modestly for most of the week (by Burning Man standards, anyway), but the day before, she had visited Glitter Camp and gotten blasted from head to toe, turning herself into a walking Academy Awards statue.

She slipped into bed and embraced me, nothing but glitter and a small pair of black panties between us. We started to kiss, and the mushrooms amplified the contact, each touch releasing a ripple of tingles. We buried ourselves beneath my sleeping bag, despite the heat. It was as much privacy as we could get in a yurt that contained three other people.

Right at the precipice of sex, Alenka said she didn't want to go all the way, which was fine with me. The touching, cuddling, and staring into each other's eyes were intense enough. We fell asleep sharing a pillow, our bodies intertwined, the mushrooms giving us kaleidoscope dreams.

A couple hours later we got up. On my way to the bathroom, Puffin stopped me and pulled my shirt up, revealing a streak of gold on my chest.

"You've got a bit of glitter on you, mate," he smirked.

After a day spent tearing down the camp, we went to watch the Temple burn. The atmosphere was quiet and solemn, much different from the night before. For the first time in seven days I couldn't hear any techno music and no one was dancing. The crackling of the fire was the only sound and this sad sound track meant the event I'd looked forward to for a year, and enjoyed so much, was over.

Afterward, Grant and some others headed out into what remained of Black Rock City hoping to find one last party among the ruins. I wanted to sleep. Alenka announced she was going to bed too and fell into step with me. Throughout the day, we'd interacted as we had all week, as friends, but I still held out hope we could hook up again.

"So . . . this morning was fun," she said, "but we've had such a great connection this week and I don't want to ruin the friendship."

And there it was, the classic *let's-not-ruin-the-friendship*, a defense as simple, old, and effective as a moat. My quest was officially over. I'd come to a desert-drug-orgy and I was going home without having had sex once.

Before I could respond, she spoke again.

"But, I really want to have sex."

OH MY GOD, WHAT WAS HAPPENING? For the first time in history *I don't want to ruin the friendship* was being followed by a request for sex. I was like a boxer rising off the mat in the twelfth round. *This fight's not over! The crowd is going wild as the challenger comes out swinging!*

"Well, then we should have sex," I said.

"You don't think it will ruin our friendship?"

"Those two things don't have to be mutually exclusive. Friends can have sex."

I could tell Alenka didn't totally believe me, but her horniness must have trumped her skepticism because she motioned for us to enter the yurt. Logan being asleep inside didn't stop us. We slipped underneath my shroud of invisibility (sleeping bag) and picked up where we'd left off that morning. Right as we were about to have sex, Alenka paused.

"I just want you to know," she said, "this doesn't mean anything."

Lady, I've spent the last year severing the connection between sex and emotion to an unhealthy extent, so don't worry about me.

"Yes, of course," I said, "it means nothing."

Everything; nothing; something—who cared what it "meant,"

I was finally going to have sex at Burning Man. And I knew it was going to be stupendous. Powered by the spiritual journey of the week, we'd make wild desert love for hours, barking like animals, until we climaxed in some sort of tantric orgasm explosion. NOPE! I came in less than two minutes. And she thought the sex didn't mean anything before we started.

"Are you already done?" she asked.

"It's been a long week of looking at naked women. I'm sorry."

In the morning I asked for the chance to try again, hoping to make up for my poor showing. She agreed and this time I was sure I'd be better, making love to her until the air mattress went flat, until her moans were louder than any music on the Playa, until she said, "I was wrong when I said this doesn't mean anything because it means EVERYTHING!" I was going to show her the kind of man . . . OOPS. Already done. Came even quicker the second time.

"Again?" she said. "Fuck you!"

"It's been a REALLY long week."

Luckily for me, the sex didn't end when we left Burning Man.

We stopped for the night in Reno on our way back to San Francisco. After dinner, Alenka told me she wanted to have sex again, so we retired to the room early, but discovered Logan already asleep in the other bed. Though we'd had sex in his presence twice already, it seemed weird outside Burning Man.

"I guess we can't have sex," I said.

"We can just do it in the bathroom," Alenka said.

Well, okay, then.

Only a year earlier I was a heartbroken Nice Guy. Now I was

having sex with a beautiful Eastern European girl against a bathroom counter in Reno, Nevada. I guess my plan had worked.

I lasted this time. For a while. Too long, in fact. Alenka had come several minutes earlier, but there was no end in sight for me. Though I was turned on and enjoying the sex, the physical exhaustion of the week shrouded my body like a heavy blanket and I wasn't going to finish. Not wanting to go from the guy-who-came-too-early to the guy-who-didn't-come-at-all, I needed to do something I'd never done before: fake an orgasm.

I started by increasing the speed of my motion and saying, "I'm getting close." This was foreshadowing. I contorted my face into a look that says *I'm-smelling-something-weird-but-also-laughing-and-I'm-squinting-because-it's-bright-in-here-and-oh-boy-this-roller-coaster-is-fun-but-a-little-scary-too.* You know, that kind of look. Next, I shook my body, as if I'd touched an electric fence, and let out a sound one might describe as "baboon hailing a cab."

When I'd finished my little performance Alenka peeked back over her shoulder at me. She knew something had happened, either an orgasm or a minor seizure.

"Did you finish?"

I nodded. She'd bought it.

———

Alenka had a few days before her flight home and decided to spend them with me in Los Angeles. During the drive down to LA, Alenka and I talked about sex and relationships and she revealed I was the first nonboyfriend she'd had sex with.

We spoke about our past relationships and what we were looking for. It was easy to be open, honest, and affectionate, as this was another Relationship with an Expiration Date, like the one I'd had with Simone in New York. I told Alenka about being dumped and the subsequent dating experiment. She spoke of a recently broken off engagement and a desire to rethink her approach to relationships.

"Maybe I should try being a slut like you," she said.

———

Alenka had never been to Los Angeles and wanted to see the city, but over the next three days we hardly left my apartment. I more than made up for my two pitiful performances in the yurt.

"I'm glad they weren't all as quick as the first time," she said, "though perhaps I would have seen more of Los Angeles."

In between trips to the bedroom, I had to catch up on work. As I went through the hundreds of emails I'd missed, Alenka would sit on my couch, often naked, calling friends and family or watching TV. Being back at my desk, dealing with used furniture, was a rude awakening, but having her to look at between tasks eased the withdrawal.

On the night before she was to depart, I told her I wanted to take her out to dinner at one of my favorite restaurants.

"Like on a real date?"

"A real-deal date."

She claimed it was only the second "real date" of her life and set about getting ready. When she emerged from the bathroom, she looked like a different person, a stunner in makeup, heels, and a dress. I dressed up too, in a blazer and tie. After a week of weird dusty clothes in the desert, neither of us could believe how good we looked. As we sipped our nightcap after dinner, Alenka thanked me for the special bond we'd formed.

"I've never had an adventure like this," she said. "I didn't know such a relationship was possible."

Neither of us had ideas about staying together long-distance. Though we got along well and had good sexual chemistry, we weren't in love. We were friends who had sex and it was exactly what we both wanted. Like Burning Man itself, the finite nature of our time together had made it special. We toasted to not having ruined the friendship.

The next day, we drove to the Griffith Observatory, so she wouldn't be a total failure as an LA tourist, and then headed to the airport. Because of traffic, our goodbye was rushed. No long speeches, no promises to stay in touch, just one last kiss, a wave, and she was gone through the sliding door.

In the past ten days I'd tried drugs, fallen in love with a man, seen a motorized cupcake, and had a lot of sex. Quite an adventure. I mean, yes, it would have been cool to get involved with a fuck-pile, but overall, a great experience.

Part III

AM I THE SLEAZY GUY?

17

WHY QUIT WHEN YOU'RE AHEAD?

After Alenka departed, I was left to face the consequences of my revelry. I'd lost five pounds and was suffering occasional bouts of vertigo, due to mild dehydration. My sunburned skin was starting to peel and a sleep deficit had me yawning every fifteen minutes. I barely left my apartment as I dealt with a weeklong hangover.

When I recovered, the Bros' Brunch reconvened and I told Kurt and Evan all about Burning Man, sparing only the details about my relationship with Brian (no need to make them jealous). When I'd finished, I asked what they'd been up to.

"Not much," Evan said.

"I went home with a girl from a bar last week," Kurt reported. "That was fun. Probably won't see her again. But, in other news, I got a new meditation pillow—it's great!"

Kurt proved once again he was the wisest of us all.

"So, Burning Man was the end of your self-imposed year of being single," Evan said. "Are you going to try to find a relationship now?"

During my recovery week, I'd thought this over. Was it time to move past all this, to settle back down? I was in my thirties, after all. In my hometown, bachelors over thirty had to wear a red *B* on their chest so they could be easily identified and set up with someone's niece.

But I lived in LA, where being single in your thirties wasn't weird. In fact, it was an advantage. Unmarried, gainfully employed, nonasshole guys over the age of twenty-eight were valuable commodities. But wanting to stay single wasn't just about being a scarce resource; I also felt more confident than I ever had.

For the first time in my life I didn't feel like a boy playing an adult in a high-school play. I lived alone, cooked for myself, could afford premium cable, owned blazers, and washed my sheets on a regular basis. With a Gentleman Résumé like this, I expected to be knighted any day.

"I'm at the height of my powers," I told the guys. "Why would I give up casual dating?"

"For love or companionship or true intimacy?" Evan said.

As I dipped my French toast into cinnamon guava syrup, I waved him off.

"Who needs those dumb things?"

———

Because I'd let relationships lapse as I prepared for Burning Man, I had to start with a clean slate. Expecting the usual low response rate, I messaged a dozen women at once. Because of luck or improved technique, I got several responses and ended up with three first dates on three consecutive nights.

A year earlier, this would have seemed an impossible task. Back then I had needed at least forty-eight hours of mental prep before each date to harden my psyche against nervousness and possible rejection. But now I wasn't anxious at all. I knew what to wear, where to go, the pathos to emote, and the jokes to tell. Dating was now like building an IKEA desk, simple and easy, with a successful end product almost assured.

Three nights in a row I went to a different bar and met a different girl and had the same experience: The same awkward hello; the same discussion of childhood, families, and hometowns; the same explanation of career, goals, and frustrations; the same hugs goodbye and proclamations of "This was fun we should do it again"; the same follow-up texts.

I didn't experience amazing chemistry with any of the girls, but that was okay. I'd become so good at mimicking what it's *like* to connect that I didn't need to *actually* connect anymore. I could create a successful date by recognizing patterns and reacting to them.

PATTERN RECOGNIZED: Date opens up about family.
RUN PROGRAM: Talk about parents' divorce and seem vulnerable.
PATTERN RECOGNIZED: Date enjoys travel.
RUN PROGRAM: Tell funny story about backpacking in Europe.
PATTERN RECOGNIZED: Date is talking about profession.
RUN PROGRAM: Ask lots of questions and seem fascinated.
PATTERN RECOGNIZED: Date likes the *Twilight* series.

RUN PROGRAM: Pretend that's not ridiculous.

PATTERN RECOGNIZED: Date complains about prior relationships.

RUN PROGRAM: Tell story that shows I've suffered similar pain, but that indicates optimism remains.

MASK DATA: Possible emptiness of soul.

A lot of people, maybe even most, dislike dating, but I loved it. After my three dates in three nights, I finally understood why: the charge I was getting from dating was very similar to the one I got from performing live. In both cases I was seeking validation by persuading strangers to like me using a well-practiced routine. As a comedian, the validation came in the form of laughter; with women, in getting a second date.

This realization gave me pause. Just as there's something unnatural about wanting to perform in front of strangers (it's many people's greatest fear), maybe dating so much was abnormal too. Maybe it was a defense mechanism. After all, if you're no one's boyfriend, you can't be anyone's ex-boyfriend. For the first time, I wondered if my "experiment" might be unhealthy. Was I changing my relationship pattern or just filling a void with the affection of strangers?

Well, no time to contemplate that now—I had three second dates to go on!

The word *casual* in *casual dating* implies it is easy and laid-back, but the opposite is true. To do casual dating properly, one must be disciplined and organized.

Keys for dating several people at once:

- **DO** remember that continuity matters—If you can't see someone often, stay in touch. No contact at all for over a week will kill most relationships.

- **DON'T** just text—In a world of text messaging, a phone call feels special. *A phone call? My, my, this thoughtful person must have been trained in Britain's most prestigious politeness school!* Plus, phone calls get you a quick answer so you can move on to the next person if the first is busy.

- **DO** make definitive plans—When dating multiple people there can be no "we should get together sometime this week." That's how you end up with scheduling conflicts. Find out what night your date is free and schedule a specific event and time. This has the added bonus of showing decisiveness.

- **DON'T** make booty calls—Unless it's been explicitly discussed that the relationship is sex-only, nobody likes to feel like they're only being contacted because of horniness. Make plans that involve more than having sex (even if you'll mostly be having sex).

- **DO** own two sets of sheets—I know this one is kind of scumbaggy, but it's a good tip. For both sanitary and aesthetic reasons. Sometimes you might not have time to do a load of laundry between dates.

- **DON'T** make a spreadsheet—At times it will be tempting. Keeping everything straight will be difficult, but remember, turning people into data points is never a good idea.

- **DO** protect your phone—Set your phone so it locks and there are no previews of texts or emails. Sure, both people might know it's a casual fling, but breaking the fourth wall will ruin the mood.

On my string of second dates I had a hard time keeping things straight. *Who was the assistant at the production company? Was it Brenda or the other brunette I took to the cocktail bar? And which one did I kiss? I'm almost certain I kissed one of them.* It was a microcosm of my whole dating experience—everything was starting to blend together.

The second dates all went well, but one stood out. At the end of the night, the short brunette, Brenda, invited me to her apartment, but prefaced the invite by saying, "Nothing's going to happen." This wasn't the first time I'd heard this phrase during my dating time. What "Nothing's going to happen" means is "Everything's going to happen except actual intercourse."

At the height of a heated, mostly naked makeout session, while caught up in the moment, I blurted out something I never thought I'd say.

"When we have sex I'm going to fuck you so hard."

WHO HAD I BECOME? Who talks like that except a private detective in a Cinemax soft-core porn?

I nearly apologized right after I said it. I'd always tried to be a Nice Guy not only on "the street," but also "between the sheets." Brenda didn't seem to mind, though—she kissed me harder and the intensity of our session increased. I became forceful in my actions and she matched my roughness at every turn.

When I'd started my year of dating I'd believed women should be treated delicately during sex, as if made of papier-mâché. This belief stemmed from movies, which had convinced me as a young-ster that the ultimate in sexual romance for a woman was slow and gentle lovemaking on a bed of roses. But for Brenda, passion and assertiveness trumped politeness.

At the end of the night, as I kissed her goodbye, Brenda grinned and said, "You're trouble." This made me feel very cool.

That's right, lady, I'm trouble. Sexy Trouble. Yeah, I'm the kind of trouble that sticks with you, that don't wash off with soap. No, you're going to need a scalding hot bath with baking soda to get rid of this trouble. Wait, maybe now I'm describing poison oak? Anyway, you get the picture. I was TROUBLE.

Brenda asked when we could go out again.

"We'll see," was all I said, because Trouble don't stick to a sched-ule. But, then again, Trouble did have to take his Volkswagen Jetta in for service next week, which would complicate things. Might be best for Trouble to pencil something in.

The next time I saw Brenda it was part of a different kind of back-to-back than my three dates in three nights—I had sex with different women on consecutive nights. Brenda was the first, fol-lowed the next night by Sonya, the girl I'd been with when I ran into Kelly. I had to admit that it thrilled me a bit, to be this "good" at getting girls, but with the excitement came qualms. Though I'd made no promises of exclusivity to either woman, they'd probably be bothered by what I'd done. Plus, feeling prideful about it felt icky. These were people I was dating, not achievements to unlock in a video game. Was it possible to be too good at dating?

18

A FEW RED FLAGS

We all have emotional baggage; it's nothing to be ashamed of. The bad things that happen to us and the poor decisions we make may shape us, but they don't have to define us. But, broadcast problems too soon and they become Red Flags. A girl I was dating, Wendy, had more Red Flags than a Chinese military parade:

- At age twenty-nine, she was currently living with her mother. RED FLAG
- She became blackout drunk on almost a weekly basis. RED FLAG
- She brought up and talked about—at length—not one but two ex-boyfriends. RED FLAG
- She had moved in with one of the ex-boyfriends after a week of dating him and he turned out to be gay. RED FLAG.
- She dated the other ex-boyfriend for over a year despite its being an extremely volatile relationship. RED FLAG
- She readily admitted she was not over her last boyfriend. RED FLAG

If Wendy and I had been together for six months by the time I heard all this, I wouldn't have cared. But we hadn't been together for six months. We hadn't been together for six hours. She revealed all of this on our first date. Which wasn't even a date.

I'd run into Wendy at a hipster dance club in Silver Lake, where, instead of velvet ropes, bottle service, and techno, they have skinny jeans, PBR, and mash-ups of Vampire Weekend. Wendy and I knew each other, but barely, having met through friends a couple times. After a few hours of dancing, I suggested going back to my place for a drink and she accepted.

We were on my couch, sipping beers, the dance-induced sweat on our shirts still drying, when she began to unload all her Red Flags at once. It was more therapy session than conversation as everything flowed from her in a long monologue prompted by my probing question, "Where do you live?"

When she finished speaking I comforted her, told her she was a great person who deserved to be happy, and drove her home. One night of physical pleasure wasn't worth the risk of engaging with someone who had so much to sort out emotionally.

NO . . . WAIT . . . That's not what happened at all.

Instead, I waited until the conversation came to a lull and kissed her. One night of physical pleasure was TOTALLY worth whatever fallout might come. When you're not interested in a relationship, a Red Flag can look a lot like a Green Light.

The makeout session was one of the strangest I'd ever experienced, aggressive and passionate, but, at Wendy's request, fully clothed. We were doing sex positions—missionary, doggy style, reverse cowgirl—but in our clothes, practicing the Dry Hump

Kama Sutra. It was so unusual, I didn't know if I should count it as another Red Flag or not.

———

Judging by all the Red Flags, at best Wendy was a little kooky and at worst a big old pile of hot mess. After our first rendezvous I knew there was no way we'd have a serious relationship, but we had nice physical chemistry, even with our clothes on, so I asked her out again, which meant finding more Red Flags.

On our next date she told me all about how she'd once worked at a bar as a paid "date." Men would come into the club and choose a girl to be his social companion for the evening, talking to him, fetching him drinks, and dancing with him. She never had sex with a client, because she didn't want to and it was against the official rules, but other girls often did. I didn't mind that she'd had this job, but a second date is when you talk about childhood fears, not the icky feeling you got from being a pseudo sex worker. Red Flag.

After dinner we returned to my house and started fooling around, this time removing clothing. There was biting, scratching, and hair pulling, which I'd experienced before, though not with such animalistic fervor. It frightened me a bit, but excited me as well.

Wendy explained that she liked to be physically dominated in bed, but not degraded. She enjoyed dirty talk, but didn't want to be called a slut or a whore—kink without misogyny. While pinning down her hands I would think about how women deserve equal pay in the workplace.

When things got heated, Wendy pulled away.

"I'm trying to be good," she said. "I've had sex too quickly in the past and I don't want to do that anymore. How many people have you had sex with?" (Too early to be discussing this—Red Flag.)

Having almost doubled my lifetime sex number in slightly over a year, I proudly reported I'd slept with thirteen people in my life.

"Yeah, see, that's barely anything. I've slept with A LOT more than that."

Wendy left late that night and after I walked her to her car, I went to the bathroom to brush my teeth. As I began brushing, I noticed something—a small bruise on my right biceps. There was another one on my shoulder. I moved my gaze from my arm to the mirror and I froze—my body was covered in dozens of hickeys.

Toothpaste dripped from my agape mouth as I examined the damage in the mirror. There were small blue bruises, crescent arches of teeth marks, and long red stripes made by fingernails. I'd known things had gotten a little rough, but this looked like I'd just gotten home from a hard day of octopus wrangling.

Normally, this wouldn't have been an issue, as they were all in places I could cover with a shirt, but I was flying to Mexico the next day for a family beach vacation. And so, at 3:00 a.m., I googled "How do you get rid of hickeys?" The consensus on the internet was to alternate between using ice (to reduce swelling) and rubbing the marks with a bare hand (to increase blood flow and reduce discoloration). I sat on my bathtub doing both things for two hours. I tried other suggestions too, such as using a hair dryer, applying a warm tea bag, and patting the hickeys with a hairbrush. It all seemed unlikely to work, but it was either this or convince my family that turtlenecks were the newest chic beachwear. *Oh yeah, the neck-du-turtle is all the rage in the French Riviera this year.*

By the time I went to bed I'd made some progress and the next morning all but a persistent few had faded. My dad commented on one, but I blamed it on getting hit with a racquetball, and though it wasn't 1988, he bought it.

These are the kind of things you deal with when you ignore Red Flags.

———

Of course, that didn't stop me from seeing her again. But after a couple more dates, Wendy did something REALLY crazy. She told people we were dating.

I ran into a mutual friend at a bar and he asked if we were together.

"She told me all about the dates you've been going on," he said. "She seemed excited, like you were practically her boyfriend."

Biting, conversations about ex-boyfriends, weird naked kissing parties without sex—this was all passable. Telling people we were a couple—over the line! How DARE a girl I'd gone out with several times think we might be headed toward a relationship? This girl was CRAZY, right? This was a total RED FLAG.

But of course she wasn't acting crazy. We got along and had good physical chemistry—things HAD gone well between us. Being excited and telling people about the relationship was natural. That's how dating works. If anyone was acting "crazy," it was I. I'd seen all of Wendy's Red Flags, but what about my own?

- Seeking self-validation by getting girls. RED FLAG
- Dating a girl despite having had no intention of a serious relationship. RED FLAG

- Willingness to have a fling with a woman in a vulnerable place because I wanted sex. RED FLAG
- Judging a girl for doing everything but sex, while knowing I probably would have stopped seeing her once we had sex. RED FLAG
- Telling my friends about the "crazy" girl who'd bitten me all over, despite having liked it in the moment. RED FLAG

I'd believed I could ignore Wendy's Red Flags because I wasn't looking for a girlfriend, but I should have seen her Red Flags as a sign that I needed to be extra honest about my intentions. But I didn't. And that was the biggest Red Flag of all. I didn't ask her out again.

19

DATING AFTER
THE EXPIRATION DATE

In New York, the parameters of my relationship with Simone had been clear: a short fling between strangers that was over when I left. Her coming to see me in LA meant it was no longer that simple. Maybe we'd have another week of carefree sex, but it was also possible that for Simone, this trip was a relationship scouting expedition.

At first it seemed like my worries were misplaced. I picked up Simone from the airport, we stopped by my house for a quick sex session, and then I dropped her off at her friend's place. Maybe she really was in LA to see her good friend and the trip didn't "mean" anything. I relaxed. Between her lady lunches, best-friend gab sessions, and pillow fights, I probably wouldn't even see Simone much. I would just give her rides and have sex with her, like a sexual-Uber.

On the second day, when I picked her up for dinner, she was waiting on the front stoop of her friend's house with her suitcase.

"I thought I'd stay over at your place tonight. That okay?"

"Of course," I said as I grabbed the bag.

When she unpacked all of her things it became clear she'd be with me for the rest of her trip. "It would be great to see you when I'm in town" had become "I'll be staying with you for almost a fortnight."

Oh, you poor baby, a pretty girl traveled to Los Angeles and you had to have sex with her for eleven days. I know. I really am a whiny bitch. And we did have fun during her visit. I played tour guide, showing my favorite spots in Los Angeles, taking her on a new "date" every night, dates I could fully enjoy because I didn't have to focus on "doing well." She'd come three thousand miles to see me; I'd already "done well."

The prolonged stay created a level of intimacy I didn't get from my normal, purposefully shallow relationships, and as the visit progressed, it became clear Simone would be open to moving to Los Angeles if I asked. She kept mentioning things she loved in LA: the weather, the proximity to her best friend, the more-laid-back vibe. It would be easy to transfer to her company's LA office, she assured me.

Though being separated by three thousand miles might have seemed daunting, Simone had her parents' marriage as an example of how this model of dating could be successful. Her father had met her mother on vacation and they were long-distance for a couple years before marrying—*uh-oh, that sounded a lot like us.*

From the way she told their story, I could tell I wasn't the only one attracted to the Grand Romantic Narrative. Simone wanted the big story, the one where I, the dedicated bachelor, declared my love and asked her to move across the country to be with me. She wanted the Fairy Tale. I even started to wonder if this was the very ending I was looking for.

On a cloudless day toward the end of her stay, we drove up the coast to a Malibu beach. It was too cold to get in the water, but warm enough to be in swimsuits, and Simone looked great in her blue-and-white polka-dot bikini. We passed a ripe peach back and forth, alternating bites, silently enjoying each other's company. It felt like we were a real couple. I could see myself with Simone, could see how we might make for a great pairing.

Though I'd focused more on the physical part of my mission (clearly), I had been thinking about the future too, even compiling a list of traits I wanted in a girlfriend. The purpose of this list was to guard against unwise emotional decisions. It's easy to know when you're in love—you just feel it. What's not so easy is separating those feelings and judging whether the person will be an objectively good life partner. I hoped by creating this list before I got into a relationship, I'd have a blueprint uninfluenced by love and infatuation.

Here was The List so far:

• **Has her shit together**—This meant having a full-time job (ideally, a career), a living situation with less than two roommates, and no outstanding warrants. A surprisingly high bar in Los Angeles.

• **Low-maintenance**—This is a pretty standard request, but something to which I needed to pay attention. High-maintenance people held allure for me because maintaining something made me feel needed. But a long-term partner should make one's life easier, not harder.

• **Has long-term important friendships/relationships**—It's a bad sign if a person you want to date can't maintain a long-term relationship. I vowed to take heed if a woman was not in touch with anyone from her past and had fallen out with several former "best friends." It might mean I'd be next on the falling-out list.

• **Like AND love?**—In a relationship it's important to not just love the person but to like them too. Seems self-explanatory, but sometimes I'd found it hard to judge if I'd be friends with a person if I weren't having sex with them. If a wizard cast a spell that made me unable to have sex ever again, would I still enjoy hanging out with my girlfriend? If no, then I shouldn't date her. (I know what you're thinking, but no, a counterspell won't work in this situation. The wizard has a staff made of dragon bone, so there's no possible defense.)

• **Truly respect my partner**—In the past, when faced with a problem, I'd often think, *I won't bother my partner with this issue*, figuring their reaction would only cause me more stress. Not believing my partner to be someone capable of helping me through a difficult time meant I didn't really respect her or her input.

I realize this isn't exactly a groundbreaking list, but it was important for me to put these things on paper. I needed to be thoughtful about what I ultimately wanted, so love couldn't blind me to seemingly obvious issues, as had happened in the past.

Simone passed all of the requirements for an objectively good long-term partner. She had a great job, was socially capable and intelligent, and I genuinely enjoyed hanging out with her. No doubt about it, she was a catch. I should have wanted to be her boyfriend.

But, ultimately, I didn't. And it didn't have much to do with her—I didn't want to be anyone's boyfriend. Simone was a great person and I enjoyed my time with her, but I also looked forward to her leaving, so my life could be my own again. I wasn't ready to stop being selfish, to take on the responsibility that comes with caring about a significant other.

Though her hints about a relationship escalated through the week, we made it to the end of the trip without discussing the future. My relief was short-lived, though. Two days after leaving, she called. We'd never talked on the phone before, always exchanging text messages instead, but you need to talk to have The Talk. It took a few minutes for her to warm up to it, but then she asked about "us" and I had to explain that there was no "us." I told her I'd be happy to see her again, but I didn't want a relationship with her.

"We had such a great time while I was there," she said.

"We did."

"I don't understand."

I could see why she was confused. Spending eleven days together, having sex, being intimate, it means something. Even if you don't verbalize what exactly these things mean, they still mean *something*. Or should. But for me, they hadn't. I liked her, I'd enjoyed spending time with her, but it hadn't gone beyond that for me.

Not only was this unfair to Simone, but it made me worry about my own state. How could I go through the motions of basically being someone's boyfriend without getting attached? Staying single had started as a choice, but I began to wonder if I'd lost the ability to form a meaningful relationship. A great girl had entered my life and dating her didn't tempt me at all. Nearly a year and a half into my project, I wondered if I was making emotional progress or taking a giant step back.

20

USE OR BE USED

In the beginning of a relationship, there is "magic" in text exchanges. The rhythm and synchronicity can flow like a scene from a romantic comedy, as if each party has a gay magical woodland creature best friend helping them compose the messages.

When we'd started going out, Hattie and I had that "magic." But no more. Only logistics remained.

Hattie: *Something got canceled tonight. Want to come to my place at 6 pm?*
Me: *Cool*

SIZZLING.

When we started, I liked Hattie so much I hadn't even Plotted Points. I saw her twice the first week and on our third date I met several of her friends at a dinner party. Originally from Arkansas, Hattie had the charm of a "proper" southern woman: she wore dresses, was unfailingly polite, and never swore. But underneath the shy, sweet exterior bubbled a sexiness she couldn't hide. She had the voice of a jazz singer, soft and smoky, like her hazel eyes.

After our fast start, Hattie and I had only seen each other once in five weeks due to busy schedules. The realization that we weren't making each other a priority had ended the "magic" in our text messages. We were still open to dating, but it was clear we weren't falling in love, which sapped our enthusiasm.

On my way to her place I got another text: *Just a warning—I've got an early and long day tomorrow. Can't be up late.*

SCORCHING.

As we walked to a nearby restaurant, I put my arm around her, but she didn't squeeze closer to me. The space between us made us look like teenagers posing during a prom date. I let my arm drop after a few paces.

The sushi place, which had dirty carpet, faded decor, and poorly translated menus, felt like the ultimate "Plan B" restaurant. It was a perfect metaphor for our once promising relationship, now alive only because of convenience. The food was bad and our conversation worse. Not having seen each other for several weeks, we should have had a lot to talk about, but we both defaulted to "not much."

We began kissing almost as soon as we returned to her apartment. Our ability to make small talk had vanished, but physically we could still hold a conversation. We gripped each other with desperation, trying to smother the unease between us. Our emotional needs weren't being met, but passion could make us forget we had those needs, for a little while, anyway.

Afterward, as the chemicals of sex receded, the remoteness

returned. We lay near each other, not touching, like siblings forced to share a bed while visiting Grandma. Yawns and mentions of how busy she was the next day were her only contribution to our post-coital conversation. I finally got the hint.

"Should I head home so you can get some sleep?"

"I guess so." She tried to sound like she regretted what she'd probably hoped for from the beginning.

As she watched me get dressed, I had a feeling I'd never had before—I felt cheap. She'd fit me into her schedule not because she wanted to see me again, but so she could get laid, and now she was sending me out into the cold night. (Since I lived in Los Angeles, not actual cold—it was sixty-eight degrees—but like *emotional* cold.)

Despite it being 11:45 p.m., I hit traffic on the drive home, because there is always traffic in LA. As I sat there not moving on the 101, I got angry. There was no way around it—Hattie had used me. She'd used me for my body and then thrown me away like a half-eaten candy bar. *Well, you know what, lady? I'm not filled with nougat—I'M FILLED WITH EMOTIONS.*

I hoped she knew she'd missed out on some GREAT cuddling. I had my cuddle game on lock: always willing to be the big spoon, eager to dole out back rubs, happy to talk about hopes and dreams. Not to mention my soft skin! With me, you're not getting the reptile skin of a philistine who doesn't believe in moisturizing. No, I am a daily user of lotion, and YOU reap the benefits.

As I stared into the glowing red taillights in front of me, I hatched my plan. I would put on a full-bore assault of woo to win this girl's heart. There would be no more occasional check-ins—I was going to call often for long and engaging conversations. And there would be flowers and trinkets and little gifts. And next time we had sex I wouldn't stop until she'd had a billion orgasms. Afterward, we'd embrace so warmly she'd think, *Inside these magic cuddle arms is the only place I feel safe in the world!*

I was going to do everything someone does when they want to be a girl's boyfriend. Everything, of course, except be her boyfriend. No, once I'd wooed her, and it was time to have The Talk, well, let's just say she'd be the one sitting in traffic late at night.

Nobody puts Matteson in the corner.

———

"I don't know why you're so mad. Isn't this what you wanted?" Kurt asked the next day as I ate brioche French toast with banana citrus caramel topping.

He was right. Sex without commitment was exactly what I'd signed up for.

"Yeah, if anything, I would have thought you'd feel proud," Evan said.

Hey, yeah, I should have felt proud! A woman with a busy schedule had wanted sexual pleasure and she'd called upon me to provide it. *Need a break from the go-go lifestyle of the modern woman? Feel free to use my sexual prowess to take your mind off Having-It-All.*

I realized the problem—while I didn't want a girlfriend, I wanted to be with women who wanted to be my girlfriend. I wanted to be wanted. It sucks to reject people, but it sure beats being rejected.

"Also, I think your dating success may be going to your head a bit," Evan added.

I hated to admit it, but the ego bruise probably was a big part of it. *How could Hattie reject me, the King of Dating?* It was an unhealthy attitude. I'd have to be careful about that.

Evan had some news of his own to share.

"So, Joanna is back in the picture. She wrecked her car last week."

"And it was Evan to the rescue?" Kurt asked.

"She called me. Very upset of course. Needed a sympathetic ear. We're not back together, but we've talked or texted almost every day. I may go visit her."

Evan held his coffee cup in front of his face, a shield against our disapproving stares. But neither Kurt nor I said anything. We'd said it all before. Maybe the sixth time would be the charm.

As for Hattie and me, we never saw each other again. I texted her a couple of weeks later, having come to terms with my status as a sentient sex toy, but she didn't respond. After being angry she'd used me, I was of course mad that she no longer wanted to use me.

21

THE SLEAZY GUY

A lot of people leave the club drunk. That's not special. But arriving at the club wasted? At only 8:30 p.m.? THAT takes work. I achieved this feat by attending a three-hour beer festival before going to the club. I'd started out thinking things like *My, my, I don't think I've ever tried a Saison so delicate! Do I detect rosemary?* By the end of the session, my analysis had simplified to *THIS BEER IS BEER FLAVORED AND IT IS GETTING ME FUCKED UP!*

Drunk and randy after the beer festival, I decided to fish at a pond where I'd had luck before, the same hipster dance club where I'd met Red Flag. Because I arrived early the dance floor was sparse, but I didn't mind. In fact, I enjoyed having the space to fully express myself.

As the night wore on, the dance floor filled with people, many of them pretty women. As I danced, I scanned for an interested party and eventually caught eyes with a pretty redhead. Back in the ancient days (fourteen months earlier), making eye contact with women was a herculean feat. I'd either look away instantly, betraying my lack of confidence, or stare too long and seem like a creep.

I'd since improved. I held eye contact with the redhead for a beat, just long enough to let her know it was intentional, and then looked away before it changed from *I'm interested* to *I'm interested in cutting off your hair and eating it.*

It worked and we began to dance near each other. It was on. But I wasn't ready to make the final move. I had more pressing needs—another drink. If there's one thing drunk people know for sure, it's that they're not drunk enough. While waiting in line for my drink I felt a tap on my shoulder; it was the girl from the dance floor.

"You left me out there," she said.

"I'm sorry. Can I make it up to you by buying you a drink?"

"How about a shot?"

Exactly what someone who's been drinking for five hours needs—I ordered tequila.

We returned to the dance floor together. I put my hands on her hips and drew her close.

"Finally!" she whispered into my ear.

Normally, I would never use the term "sucking face," because it is the grossest possible name for kissing, but it is the best way to describe what we were doing. Our mouths were wide open, our tongues flapped around like two spasming fish, and there was a loud smacking sound, like when a dog is trying to get peanut butter off the roof of its mouth. Yep, we were definitely sucking face. Our hands were all over each other too. She initiated the first contact, guiding my palm to her ass, and then, later, placing my hand on her breast.

This went on for several songs, but then she disappeared. One second we were making out like nineteen-year-olds in Cancún and the next I was humping air. I looked around, but a strobe light made it hard to see. Where'd she go? I pushed through the crowded dance floor trying to find her. After a couple minutes I spotted her off to the side, surrounded by friends—they must have pulled her away. I locked eyes with my dance partner and she beckoned me over, but when I tried to approach, a short blonde stopped me with a scowl.

"Stay away from her, you sleaze," she spat, before spiriting my dance/face-suck partner away to the women's room.

I was stunned. A sleaze? Me? IMPOSSIBLE. How could I be a sleaze? I was shy in high school!

Sure, our physicality was a bit over the top, but the girl I'd been allegedly sleazing drove the behavior. She'd followed me off the dance floor. She'd suggested shots. She'd said, "Finally," when I put my hands on her. If anything she took advantage of poor innocent me. There I was, expressing myself through the art of dance, when she made me touch her boobs and butt.

Plus, was it *that* bad, what I was doing with . . .

Shit . . .

I didn't know her name. You should probably know someone's name *before* you know what her tongue tastes like. That was a bit sleazy, I had to admit.

Back in college, I'd often been on the other side of this equation. While we were out at the bars, my friend Tanya would get drunk, inevitably start dancing with some weird guy, and my college girlfriend, Maria, would get me to go "rescue" Tanya by pulling her over to dance with us. It wasn't that the guy was being horrible or that Tanya wasn't complicit, but Maria could tell Tanya would regret hooking up once sober.

I was now the potential regret from which a girl needed rescuing. I hadn't harassed the redhead or done anything "wrong," but you don't have to be doing something malicious to be sleazy. And now that I thought about it, some of my other behavior that evening had been unseemly too. I'd been texting, or more accurately, sexting, with two girls at once. I'd even reused messages, copying from one conversation and pasting into the other. The needle of the Sleaze-o-meter was swinging dangerously close to the red.

But that wasn't all.

I'd also texted a third girl, my Fuck Buddy, and invited her to the club. So, I'd been making out with the redhead to kill time before another girl arrived. Classy. And when the FB did arrive, I acted out the same script, dancing and kissing her aggressively.

"Let's take it down a notch in public," my FB said as she pulled away. Being too aggressive for a Fuck Buddy? That's definitely sleazy.

I'd started my mission with such high aspirations, wanting to learn about the modern state of dating and explore my own feelings when it came to relationships. I had planned to interact with women honestly and leave both of us satisfied, physically and emotionally. It had even worked for a while. Most of the people I'd dated had enjoyed our time together and I felt I'd grown as a person.

But that night at the club, my virtuous aims had fallen by the wayside. And it wasn't an isolated incident—this had been happening for months. Honesty had taken a backseat to getting laid. Figuring out what traits I wanted in a long-term partner no longer mattered—figuring out how to get another girl in my bed did. I had shed my Nice Guy baggage, but I'd gone too far in the other direction. I was the adult equivalent of the bra snappers I'd hated so much in junior high.

I was now the Sleazy Guy.

The next morning, after my FB left, I could barely get to brunch I felt so sick. Yes, 90% of it was the massive hangover caused by ten straight hours of drinking, but the other 10% was something else, something that couldn't be placated by eggs and sausage (not even farm fresh eggs and chicken-basil-cracked-pepper sausage). Beyond the headache and queasiness, I was ashamed of how I'd behaved. I didn't want to be the Sleazy Guy.

"I think I'm done with casual sex," I told the guys at Bros' Brunch. "No more flings. I'm officially looking to date girls I could have a real relationship with."

"End of an era," Kurt said. "End of a slutty, slutty era."

"Speaking of an end of an era," Evan said, "I think I'm done with Joanna."

Evan was supposed to be in Salt Lake City that weekend, but the trip had gotten canceled. Two days before he was supposed to arrive, Joanna had asked him not to come because she was "confused about her feelings." The next day she had changed her mind, apologized, and asked him to come after all. But it was too late— Evan no longer wanted to go.

"I just don't think I can do it anymore. When things are good between us, they're so good, and I keep waiting for her life to settle, but it may never happen. I think I have to accept that this is what our relationship is and it's probably not going to change."

This was good news from my point of view, but I could tell Evan felt down, so I wasn't sure whether to offer condolences or congratulations (condolulations?). Kurt and I told him we were proud of him for making a firm decision, though I think we both secretly wondered if this break would actually stick. We'd heard the "I'm done with Joanna" speech before.

22

CAN WE HAVE SEX
BEFORE THE FIRST DATE?

So, I know I just said I would stop my philandering and start looking for a relationship. And I meant it. But then I got this text message: *Do you think we could have sex before the first date? Everyone
says not to have sex on a first date, but no one says anything about
BEFORE the first date.*

I mean, how could I turn that down?

I told her I was intrigued. She said she'd be at my place in ninety
minutes.

What harm could one more bout of meaningless sex do?

———

Our mutual friend Emory, whom I had performed with at a couple
shows, had set me up with Lillie. She looked cute in pictures and
seemed brilliant—she had a PhD in physics—so I'd given Emory
the go-ahead.

Two weeks earlier, Lillie had sent an email inviting me to go
hiking. Normal. Except the hike she proposed was in Arizona and
would take place in four months. Not so normal. Lillie wanted

me to come with her to a natural attraction in Arizona called The Wave. Only twenty hikers were allowed in per day, and she'd won a ticket through a lottery system. It did sound cool, but a long weekend in another state seemed a bit much for a first date. I suggested we meet for a drink so we could get to know each other and I could learn more about the trip.

But a few days before the scheduled date, she sent me that text, and now a stranger was on her way to deliver me sex as if it were a pizza. The only thing that could make it better was if she also brought a pizza.

But I was nervous. What was I supposed to do when she arrived? She was coming over explicitly for sex, but should I offer her a drink and get to know her first? Or was I supposed to pull her inside, throw her on the ground, and ravage her with my passion?

Her knock was shy, almost inaudible. I opened the door. She wore a yellow dress that hung loosely over her petite body. She was smiling meekly. I invited her inside and decided against the instant ravaging, instead making us drinks. Small talk quickly gave way to silence. We'd called each other's bluff on this sex-before-the-first-date thing and neither of us knew how to act. Before she'd arrived, this had felt like a situation out of a porno movie, but the awkwardness was not like a porno movie. This was more like a scene from a black-and-white Nordic film about the loneliness of the human condition.

Lillie took charge, grabbing my shirt and pulling me toward her. After a few minutes of kissing she stood up.

"Can we go to your bed now?"

I nodded.

"Unzip me," she said once we were in the bedroom. I helped her remove her dress and then took off my clothes. From strangers to naked in fifteen minutes, a new record for me. We got into my bed and after a few minutes of kissing I fished a condom out of my nightstand.

"So soon?" she asked.

Apparently, I was the one in a hurry now.

"There's no rush," she said, "we have all night."

I didn't know we had "all night." When she'd texted me, I assumed it would be a fast, passionate encounter, possibly over in an hour. Porno movies don't last all night.

We kept fooling around until she pulled away, mid-kiss, and said, "You're a screenwriter, right? What happens when you finish a screenplay? How does it become a movie?"

A Hollywood Q&A session at this point seemed odd, but if "odd" were a problem, we wouldn't have gotten this far. With her lying naked on top of me, I explained the inner workings of the film industry.

The rest of our foreplay session went on in this manner, alternating between physical interplay and chitchat. While kissing my neck, she told me about her favorite TV show (*House*) and in the middle of giving me a hand job she asked how many siblings I had. Combining awkward first-date small talk with hooking up was strange. It's weird to be telling someone where you were born while you're fingering them.

With no warning, Lillie took hold of my penis and started to put it inside her.

"I need to get a condom," I said, twisting away from her.

"We don't need that," she said.

I am a safe sex advocate. I believe you need "that" whenever you engage in nonmonogamous sex. I especially believe you need "that" when having nonmonogamous sex with a stranger. And I doubly-super-especially think you need "that" when the stranger says, "We don't need that." I reached for the condom.

Our interactions thus far had led me to believe she was assertive and sexually experienced, but the actual sex told a different story. She lay beneath me, silent and unmoving, giving no signs of enjoyment. It was just a biological act, barely pleasurable for either of us.

When we'd finished, the passivity she'd had during intercourse disappeared. She cuddled up next to me, nestling her head in the crook between my arm and chest and wrapping her legs around my hips, clinging to me like a baby koala. Her skin was warm and soft, but the contact felt forced and strange, too intimate.

"I got my driver's license last week," she said suddenly.

WHAT THE FUCK? HOW OLD IS THIS GIRL? Was the sex so unremarkable because I was having sex with an underage virgin? I sprang up in bed, shoving her off of me.

"How old are you?" I demanded.

"Thirty."

I let out a sigh as I settled back onto my pillow, relieved that the crew of *To Catch a Predator* wasn't about to burst into the room.

"I've always lived in cities where I didn't need to drive," she explained, "so I never got a license. I still don't have a car."

"How'd you get here, then?"

"I took the bus."

In an evening filled with odd behavior, not having a car in LA was the strangest yet. Public transit in Los Angeles is like an urban legend. It seems made up to scare people out of driving drunk. No wonder she'd said *We have all night*—she had no way of getting home.

As we talked, I found her evasive when I touched on certain subjects.

"Emory said he met you at a storytelling show?" I asked.

"I don't want to talk about that."

"What made you invite me on the hiking trip in Arizona?"

"I can't say. Emory might tell you."

"How do you know Emory?"

"LONG story. I'd rather not talk about Emory."

"Did you used to date him or something?"

She peered at me for a moment, unsure if she should answer, and then it all came gushing out.

"A year and a half ago I saw a video of Emory performing on YouTube. I was spellbound and watched the video over and over again. I was just drawn to him. I started attending storytelling shows and eventually I met him. He had a girlfriend, but we started up an email correspondence. A few months later he became single and we went on a date—hiking and dinner. It was an incredible day, like being on drugs, pure euphoria. But I didn't hear from him the next day or that week. I went into withdrawal. I could barely function. I needed my drug again, another Emory fix. He moved to New York and I visited him twice, but he wouldn't let me stay with him, wouldn't even invite me up to his apartment, only meeting me for lunch or dinner. Emory got a new girlfriend, but I kept emailing and calling him because I knew we were meant to be together. I said yes to going on a date with you because Emory has a way of getting me to do things."

This date was a setup, in every sense. Emory hadn't thought we'd be a good match; he was pushing her my way and saying, "Not it!" In over a year of dating strangers from the internet, a friend had arranged the only weird date.

I sat there in silence, not sure how to respond.

"Emory told me not to tell you any of this because it might ruin things between us. Has it?"

"I'd say my being some sort of sexual surrogate for Emory has hurt the chances of us dating seriously, yes."

"Are you angry?" she asked.

"No."

And I wasn't. My main emotion was relief. Her revelation meant I had no responsibility. After tonight, I didn't have to see her again, didn't have to have The Talk, and didn't have to feel bad about it. Mine was only a bit part in Emory's play. I went to sleep calm, knowing this would be over the next morning.

———

"You know how pets wake you up early because they need to eat?" Lillie asked.

I blinked awake and glanced at the clock. It was 5:30 a.m.

"What? Do you need food? I could make oatmeal."

"No, I want to have sex."

She (still naked) climbed on top of me. I felt myself becoming erect, but there was NO WAY. I was done being a part of this situation. *Sorry, penis, the brain's gonna apply his rarely utilized veto power.*

"I'm not up for that right now," I said.

She nodded and rolled back to her side of the bed. An hour later we got up and I drove her home. Despite the weirdness of the evening, making her take a bus at 6:30 in the morning was too cruel.

The "walk of shame" can be awkward, but it's nothing compared to a drive-her-home-through-an-hour-of-LA-traffic of shame. As we drove, I spoke as little as possible and stared straight ahead, my focus completely on the road. I kept both hands on the wheel, using the proper 10-and-2 alignment, so there'd be no chance of hand-holding.

During a red light, Lillie pointed up at a billboard advocating condom use and said, "I can't believe you like using those things."

"I don't LIKE them, but it's important to use them unless you're in a monogamous relationship."

"I don't plan on sleeping with anyone else," she said.

WHHHAAAAAAAATTTTT? Was she suggesting we were a couple? This was too much. I could no longer be polite.

"Well, I do," I said. "I'm dating other people. And I plan to continue doing so."

"That's fine," she responded.

"Yes, it is."

I pulled up to the curb outside her apartment.

"I'll see you Tuesday," she said as she stepped out of the car.

She was referring to our originally planned "first date," which I knew wouldn't happen, but I didn't need to tell her right then.

"Um, yeah, see you Tuesday," I said before speeding away.

The first text came only two hours later.

I miss you.

How could she miss me? *YOU DON'T KNOW ME, LADY!*

Though I didn't respond to any of Lillie's texts, they streamed in, dozens of them. Updates about work, her weekend plans, and

thoughts on our trip to Arizona (which I still hadn't agreed to).
Putting aside the weirdness with Emory, THIS was bizarre behavior. Didn't she know the proper protocol to follow if you like someone? Pretend you don't like them.

She seemed to believe our night together was the beginning of
an epic romance. I sent her an email explaining it was nice to meet
her, but that I didn't feel a romantic connection. I canceled our date
and suggested she find another person to take to Arizona. I was
kind, but firm, leaving no room for misinterpretation. I thought it
would put an end to the messages.

It only increased them.

My phone started buzzing and didn't stop—calls, voicemails,
text messages, emails. She asked what she'd done to anger me, offer-
ing different theories for why it hadn't gone well between us. Was
she too serious? Was she not serious enough? Was it the Emory
thing? She pleaded for me to respond, kept saying she missed me. If
I send two unanswered texts I assume the person is either uninterested or dead, and I never contact them again. But my silence had
the opposite effect on Lillie. I had to turn off my phone to get to
sleep that night and the messages kept coming through the next day.

I speculated that Emory had gotten wrapped up with Lillie by
trying to be polite and subtle, a mistake I wouldn't repeat. Ignoring
Lillie wasn't working; I had to be blunt.

Lillie,

*Our evening together did not offend me and I wasn't mad
at you, but I did not feel a strong connection, romantically or
platonically. Though it didn't help, it is not about the Emory*

thing—I just didn't feel the "spark" needed for us to date, even casually. I feel like I'm being hounded and it's making me angry. I sent you my first email as a way to kindly and honestly let you know I wasn't interested in us pursuing anything further. Please accept and respect my wishes. I think it's best if we don't hang out again, even as friends. Please stop trying to contact me.

Lillie sent me one more message.

Matteson,

    I wish you'd simply sent this email first. Me being upset is pretty natural I think and I want to talk more about this. Ignoring someone isn't a good way to communicate. But, you get your wish, I will not contact you anymore. I wish it worked out. I actually liked you.

I was tempted to write her back and say something like *If I'd gotten my wish, you wouldn't have sent this email.* Or *I know silence isn't a good form of communication, that was the point, I didn't want to communicate with you.* Or *It would be natural for you to be upset if we'd gone out MORE THAN ONCE.* But I didn't. I let it be over.

I ran into Emory a couple months later.

"So, when you set me up with Lillie, you were doing it to try to get her away from you?"

"No! I hoped you would it hit off. You two seemed like you might be a good match. I thought . . . Yes, I was trying to get her away from me. Sorry."

———

Despite all the flings I'd had, my experience with Lillie was my first true one-night stand. Before Lillie, I'd dated everyone at least a couple of times and gotten to know them a little bit. A year and a half after I'd started, I reached the logical extreme of my experiment: dating distilled down to nothing more than sex. I hadn't enjoyed it. The experience was dehumanizing for her and me. After my sleazy night at the club, I felt like I *should* change. After Lillie, I *wanted* to change.

I had moved on from my heartbreak, ditched the Nice Guy tendencies, and become "good" at dating. It was time for the next phase of The Plan. I was ready to not only have a girlfriend again, but to use what I'd learned to find the PERFECT relationship.

Part IV

THAT ONLY HAPPENS IN THE MOVIES

23

THE BEST-LAID PLANS

I didn't have to search long to find a girl to date seriously; I was already dating her. I'd gone out with Ella three times before my furtive night with Lillie. A drinks-only first date with the tall blonde had given way to a second date featuring dinner and a car makeout, which led to a third date at my apartment and sex. There weren't "fireworks," but we'd climbed the date ladder in an orderly fashion and had fun at every rung. It was nice and easy, and after Lillie, "nice and easy" sounded about right. Ella also met all the requirements of The List, so, after a couple more dates, I decided to ask her to be my girlfriend. I went into the conversation without the dread of The Talk, happy to be telling Ella I wanted to be with her exclusively, rather than the opposite. Ella agreed we made a good match and I had a girlfriend again.

Until I was free from the whirlwind of dating, I didn't realize how all-consuming it had been. Between searching for people to take on dates, researching places to take those dates, going on the dates, and thinking of ways to tell the dates I didn't want to go on another date, I'd used up most of my spare time. It felt great to take the time I'd been wasting on OkCupid and use it on more productive activities (Tumblr pages featuring puppies in hats).

After months spent complicating my life by dating multiple people at once, my relationship with Ella was straightforward. We ordered in, watched TV, drank scotch, and went out on the weekends. It wasn't thrilling, but it felt good to just spend time with someone, rather than be "on a date" with them.

We'd been together for two months when, on New Year's Eve, with the midnight balloons falling around us, Ella leaned in and said, "I love you."

I stared at her, surprised by the declaration.

"You don't have to say it back," she said, "I just wanted you to know."

I hugged her close, hoping the physical affection would make up for my lack of verbal affirmation. I didn't know if I loved her back. We had fun together, lots of laughs, and didn't fight, but I hadn't felt the powerful euphoria and excitement that usually accompany love.

But, wasn't the purpose of my mission to find a relationship not driven by infatuation? Instead of love sprung from passion, we could grow ours from a base of compatibility, friendship, and respect. No, I wasn't in love with Ella, but I could see a future where I would be, so I decided to round up my feelings. At the end of the song I whispered back, "I'm falling in love with you too."

Shortly after the New Year, Ella got an apartment down the street from mine, so we saw each other almost every day. We fell into the routine of a nice companionable relationship and for the first time in a long time, I felt content. I'd reset emotionally, reevaluated what I wanted in a partner, and found a sensible significant other with whom I could build a stable long-term relationship.

In February, I went on vacation to Thailand with Kurt and Grant. When we'd booked our tickets months earlier, the trip had been an extension of my experiment, a chance for vacation hookups, but being with Ella meant that was off the table. I didn't mind. My relationship with her was the culmination of my plan, what I'd set out to do eighteen months earlier, so missing out on some action while I traveled didn't seem like a big sacrifice.

After a few days in Bangkok and a trip to the Angkor Wat temples in Cambodia, Kurt, Grant, and I flew to the island of Ko Phangan. We booked a small hotel on a white sand beach where we each rented our own little bungalow, complete with a hammock on the front porch, for $15 per night.

Ko Phangan is known primarily for its epic full moon parties, which happen, you guessed it, every full moon. The pictures online made it look like a mini Burning Man, which of course had intrigued. Unfortunately, our travel didn't coincide with a full moon, but this turned out not to be a problem—we could go to the half-moon party instead. At some point the locals figured out tourists would pay to get drunk during any phase of the moon, so the roster expanded to four parties per month.

We rode to the half-moon party in the back of a pickup truck—what passed for a cab on the island—with about ten other people. (Not a lot of safety regulations in Thailand.) Everyone else in the truck was at least five years younger.

The party venue was somewhere deep in the jungle and consisted of several bars, at different levels, circling a dance floor situated between two hills. Hundreds of bodies, all in glowing neon shirts and body paint, lit up the basin, making a giant bowl of radioactive Lucky Charms.

We wandered onto the dance floor (or "dance ground"—there was no floor, only dirt) and quickly lost each other. A shirtless, muscular Brit grabbed me around the shoulders. His sweat, colored by body paint, dripped on my neck. He smelled of Red Bull and spray cologne.

"What are you drinking, mate?" he yelled.

"Nothing right now, just dancing."

He shook his head, offended by my answer.

"What are you drinking?" I asked.

He held up a Thai Bucket, the specialty drink of the island, and took a sip. Thai Buckets are a mixture of local rum, Red Bull, and Sprite served in an actual plastic bucket. It is the kind of drink that turns an "evening" into a "night."

"EVERYTHING!" the young Brit said. "I'm drinking everything, mate."

As I watched him stumble off, I believed him. And he didn't seem to be the only one drinking "everything." The party was full of people who were very young and very drunk. Many looked like they might be getting drunk for the first time in their life. The parties at Burning Man were wild, but the average age was around thirty-five, so it felt more responsible. The vibe at the half-moon party was less free-spirited-people-having-a-good-time and more Cancún-spring-break-Girls-Gone-Wild-frat-party.

I was wandering through the dance floor, observing the bad decisions being made around me and feeling old, when I felt a tap on my shoulder. I turned to see a beautiful girl looking down at me from an elevated platform.

"I know you," she said with a slight accent. "You're the dancer."

My stomach fluttered with recognition. The night before, Kurt, Grant, and I had shared a bottle of Thai whiskey before wandering to a beach bar. Toward the end of the night we'd met two girls, Nellie and Astrid. They were Swedish, though neither fit the typical blond-haired, blue-eyed Nordic stereotype, both being brunettes. When Grant had introduced me, Nellie had declared, "You're friends with HIM? The dancer!"

Now, while I do love dancing, I am not a good dancer. But I think I stood out because I was one of the few people at the party who was actually dancing. Every other guy was more interested in rubbing his crotch against someone. How disgusting, right? I would never do that, at least not since I had stopped being a Sleazy Guy, all the way back four months earlier.

Grant and I had chatted with the duo for only a few minutes, but long enough to learn they too would be at the half-moon party the next night. It was Nellie who tapped me on the shoulder. Astrid wasn't around.

"You want to join me up here to dance?" she asked.

"Sure!"

The small platform, about three feet off the ground, had a dozen other people on it, but there was plenty of room to dance. After a few minutes, Nellie stopped, looked at me, and laughed.

"I amuse you?" I asked.

"Yes. You really love dancing. You are a true dancing queen," she said with a smile that indicated it was a compliment.

From our elevated perch we were visible to much of the party. All eyes were on Nellie. She was energetic, sexy, and mesmerizing. Her hips moved precisely and in perfect rhythm, as if they'd been designed by NASA.

Guys buzzed around Nellie like mosquitoes circling a bug zapper, but, like the doomed insects, every one got zapped. Most only required a shake of her head; one she had to slap. A few times I offered my hand and pulled her to "safety," putting myself between her and a particularly persistent fellow. I was back on the right side of the sleazy divide.

"Where's your friend Astrid?" I asked.

"Hopefully off having fun with an American boy of her own."

American boy of her own. This implied I was Nellie's American boy and she was currently having fun with me. I'd never considered a European might have a thing for American boys, that foreign intrigue could work in the other direction. For the first time in my life I, an average-looking white boy from the middle of the country, felt exotic. I could wow her with my knowledge of casseroles and lack of knowledge about world geography.

"It's so hot," Nellie said as she looped the hem of her shirt through the collar, making a sort-of bikini top that showed off her flat stomach and sharp hip bones. I felt desire and lust like I hadn't felt for Ella, at least not like this. I put my hands on Nellie's waist. Surges of animalistic compulsion flashed through my mind: making out with Nellie in a dark corner; taking her back to my hotel; making love on a beach; abandoning Kurt and Grant and going with Nellie to her next destination; starting a new life in Sweden.

I wish I could say I resisted kissing Nellie. Wouldn't that be a nice moment for this story, real proof I'd changed and made progress? But I didn't. I kissed Nellie. It wasn't a full-on makeout, only a light peck with no tongue, prudish even by junior high standards, but it was still a betrayal.

Not long after the kiss, feeling guilty, I went to find Grant and Kurt. They were sipping beers at a table and watching a group of hulking Aussies sucking down balloons of nitrous and falling over. (There aren't a lot of safety regulations in Thailand.) As sunrise approached the crowd began to thin and those remaining were sweat-slicked and sloppy. We decided to leave.

Grant had danced with Astrid for a bit that evening and both of us wanted to say goodbye to the Swedes, but they were nowhere to be seen, probably on their way to catch the early-morning ferry, off to the next island, the next party, the next American boys. I didn't know Nellie's email, phone number, or even last name, which was probably for the best—there'd be no temptation to get in touch with her. She'd forever remain my flawless Swedish goddess, I her American dancing queen.

———

Back at our hotel I wasn't ready for bed.

"Beer on the porch?" I asked.

"Beer on the porch," Grant confirmed.

The sun had not yet risen, but it was close enough to the horizon to give us a preview. In the distance a long-tail boat, piled high with nets, cruised toward a fishing spot, kicking up a rooster tail wake in the flat turquoise water. After sipping our beers in silence for twenty minutes, I spoke.

"So, shall we pack up and follow the Swedes to Ko Phi Phi?"

Grant laughed and nodded. I was only half joking, though. I could feel disappointment in my stomach, the tug of the Grand Romantic Narrative. Part of me wanted to be impulsive, to chase after Nellie, going from bar to bar on the next island until I felt a tap on my shoulder and heard her say, "I know you." Following a girl across Thailand because you shared a moment on a dance floor—THAT'S the start to an epic love story. It would make a much better story than the one I had with Ella, which saw us meet online and date because it was sensible. No one wants to see that movie.

Being in your thirties is strange. You're not "young," but you're young enough to still desire the pleasures of youth. You're not "old," but you're old enough to understand you will one day be "old." I worried that I'd just squandered some of my dwindling supply of Youth out of loyalty to a woman I might not even love. Ella was a good choice for a partner, but was I ready to make good choices? Would I ever be?

A little sleep and a burger had me feeling better that afternoon and I was no longer considering hopping a ferry to find Nellie. She was back to being just a pretty girl, rather than a referendum on my life choices and a reminder of my mortality, and I was back to feeling optimistic about my relationship with Ella. True, I hadn't exactly aced the temptation test, but I figured sticking to a single small kiss got me at least a C–, a passing grade. I felt relieved I hadn't gone further and resolved not to put myself in a similar situation again. My brush with infidelity had galvanized my views on the relationship—I didn't want to lose Ella. I felt excited to see what our adult relationship could become.

So of course Ella dumped me two weeks later.

24

THE LETTER

"You couldn't have broken up with me BEFORE I went to Thailand?"

"Sorry," Ella said with a shrug, not knowing her poor timing had cost me a life full of Nordic sweaters and Swedish meatballs.

I'd been back ten days when Ella texted me she was coming over because we "needed to talk." This wasn't a total surprise. Since my return, she had been going out with friends more and answering my calls less. Her behavior wasn't as extreme as Kelly's had been, but it was a familiar scenario. Kissing Nellie had nothing to do with it, either, because I hadn't told Ella (or written it in an email).

That evening after work, there was a knock on my door. Ella had keys to my place, but wasn't using them. I guess she believed it proper to knock when visiting to dump someone. She started with general pleasantries about how great I was and then explained that while I was in Thailand, she didn't miss me as much as she thought she should, which had made her reconsider our relationship.

"You're such a good boyfriend on paper, but we're too similar. I don't feel challenged by you, by this relationship. I don't think we're the right match."

I didn't really understand what "not challenging" her meant, but I couldn't contradict the basic gist of what Ella was saying. Since our first date I'd known there wasn't magic between us, that ours was a relationship of the head, not the heart, but for me that's what made it appealing. For Ella it was a deal breaker.

"There's just something missing between us," she said. "I've rushed into a thing with a nice guy before and I didn't want to get too far down the road, no matter how pleasant it's been. That wouldn't be fair to you."

As my effort to save my relationship with Kelly had failed so miserably, I didn't put up much of a fight this time. After a short talk, we hugged goodbye, she walked out of my apartment, and I was single again.

I went to bed immediately. Well, after a quick Facebook search for Nellie, which yielded no results—it turns out there are a LOT of people named Nellie in Sweden. I lay in bed, unable to fall asleep, and with each flip of the pillow my anger grew.

I was angry Ella left me because I was too nice (isn't that what "not challenging" means?). Angry that she'd told me she loved me and changed her mind just three months later. Angry that the declaration of love had made me take our relationship more seriously. Angry she'd said, "I've rushed into a thing with a nice guy before," like I was just a generic step in her relationship pattern.

Maybe most of all, I was angry Ella had ruined my plan and made me a failure. Nineteen months after I'd begun, I was right back where I'd started—dumped. Didn't she understand I'd reached the redemptive-adult-relationship phase of my personal growth?

When I'm overwhelmed, I don't drink or punch things or get a hooker; I write. After a few hours of trying to sleep, I decided to compose a letter to Ella. I pounded at the keyboard, typing faster than I had since my speed test in eighth-grade typing class.

I'd never been good at expressing anger. In conversations with girlfriends or others I'd rarely even say "angry," instead opting for words like *frustrated* or *bothered,* no matter how egregious the offense. If I were to confront a carjacker I'd probably say, *I'm frustrated that you stole my car and it bothers me you used it as a toilet.*

In my eagerness to avoid feeling angry, I would delude myself into thinking I hadn't been wronged, that things were fine, which is what I'd done with both Kelly and Ella. I preferred blaming myself over getting mad at someone else because anger felt like weakness to me. It meant someone had affected me and I was no longer in control.

But I was ready to feel angry now and I poured all that emotion into the letter. I didn't want to vilify Ella or set myself up as a martyr, but I needed Ella to know she'd hurt me. I was tired of not telling people they hurt me.

I finished around four in the morning. The letter was long. Like REALLY long. Ten pages long. 2,895 words long. That's longer than several chapters in this book. It's longer than a LOT of things.

Things shorter than my email:

- The Declaration of Independence (1,323 words)—Our forefathers declared independence in half the words I needed to explain my feelies.

- Genesis: Chapter 1 (825 words)—The earth was made in about a quarter of the words it took me to say, "You hurt me."
- "The Love Song of J. Alfred Prufrock" (1,108 words)— T. S. Eliot launched modernist poetry with this master-piece that is way shorter than my explanation of how being dumped made me sad.
- The Gettysburg Address (272 words)—In a fraction of the words I needed to say, "My heart has a boo-boo," President Lincoln HEALED OUR NATION.
- For sale: Baby shoes, never worn (6 words)—Fuck you, Hemingway.

Despite the length, what I'd written felt honest and worthy of expressing. In the past, I never would have sent such an email, but I was done playing it cool and trying to "win" breakups. I hit Send and went to bed. With the venom out of my system, I fell immediately asleep.

Ella didn't write back for a couple weeks (probably because the letter took that long to read), but she did respond. Her email was much shorter than mine (somewhere between the Gettysburg Address and Genesis), and she called me out on the unnecessarily mean things I'd said, but her overall tone was thoughtful, reasoned, and kind. She closed her email by saying, *I'm sorry that I said I love you. I thought I did. But I should have thought more about it and not gotten caught up in the idea of our relationship. I'm sorry that I wasn't better.*

She was sorry. I had told Ella she hurt me and she said sorry. It was a simple thing, something taught in kindergarten, but it brought me immense relief. I hadn't known how much I needed to hear someone say my feelings mattered.

In the days following Ella's response, I felt happy and lighter, but a question lingered—why had her apology meant so much to me? Furthermore, why had I written such a screed in the first place? Ella and I had dated for less than six months and I wasn't even sure I loved her, and yet, I'd felt the need for extreme closure. It didn't make sense.

And then it dawned on me—I'd sent the letter to the wrong person. Though Ella's name was at the top, the letter was really for Kelly. It was filled with all the things I'd wanted to say to her, but never did.

I'd written Kelly a long letter toward the end, but its purpose was to save the relationship—I spoke little about the pain she'd caused me, instead focusing on how to fix what was wrong. After she dumped me, dedicated to hiding my wounds so I could "win" the breakup, I'd gone into my heartbreak recovery plan and initiated Ghost Protocol. I blocked her on social media, threw out pictures and keepsakes, and did my best to remove her from my brain. I hadn't needed to tell Kelly she'd wronged me because who was Kelly?

I'd chided and even pitied Evan for not being able to get over Joanna, but at least he was being genuine, while I was burying my emotions underneath sex and a pseudointellectual philoso-phy about dating. No matter how many women I went out with to prove I was "over" my relationship with Kelly, I hadn't been. I'd moved past wanting to be with her specifically, but that didn't mean I was over the loss of the relationship itself. By not expressing my pain during or after the breakup, I'd allowed it to fester.

Though I'd sent the letter to the wrong person (sorry, Ella!), it still worked. Just telling SOMEONE they'd hurt me allowed the anger to dissipate. It had taken more than a year and a half, almost thirty women, a few drugs in the desert, and an absurdly long email, but I had finally moved on and could see Kelly in a different light. She hadn't been a Manic Pixie Dream Girl, some damaged creature whom only I could save as part of my "hero's journey." And her breaking up with me wasn't a self-destructive wrongheaded move. She was just a girl who dumped a boy because she had fallen out of love with him. Which happens. It's really uncinematic, but it happens.

25

THE INFILTRATION
OF BROS' BRUNCH

There are only two requirements to be a part of Bros' Brunch:

1. Have a love of combining two meals into an hours-long supermeal revolving around seasonal toppings.
2. Have a penis.

That's it. Pretty simple. Or so I thought, until Evan broke the second rule by inviting a woman to join us. It seemed absurd. I mean, come on, a WOMAN? At BRUNCH? That's like a woman using a urinal—would she know what to do?

"Would people be up for splitting an order of French toast with caramelized peaches if I ordered one for the table?"

We'd barely sat down when she made this pro-level brunch suggestion. Maybe she was ready for the big leagues.

The woman in question was Laura, Evan's friend and ex, whom I'd messaged on OkCupid early in my dating process, not realizing I knew her. We'd seen each other a few times since our online run-in and she always made sure to tease both Evan and me about it.

Evan for being a cock-block, me for being the slut she was glad to have avoided.

Much of the conversation at brunch centered on me (surprise, surprise) and The Letter. I explained how it had finally given me closure on my relationship with Kelly.

"I actually think I'm ready to date for real now."

"Don't get me wrong," Evan said. "I felt bad when Ella dumped you, but part of me did think your plan came together a little TOO well."

"Well, the gods have punished me for my hubris. But maybe this time I can find a relationship with someone who doesn't need to be 'challenged.' "

Laura sat up in her chair.

"Is that what your ex said? That you didn't challenge her?"

I nodded.

"That's what my ex said to me too! Who wants to be challenged by their girlfriend? What does that mean?"

"I don't know!" I said. "I mean, isn't life challenging enough?"

"Exactly," Laura said. "That's what I think."

I'd heard about Laura's breakup, which had happened a couple months before Ella dumped me, and hers scored way higher on the misery scale. It wasn't so much losing the relationship, which was only about six months old, but how it had happened. Her boyfriend had dumped her in the middle of a work/vacation trip to Hong Kong, which Laura had paid for. She had to go from bouts of crying and fighting to fancy dinners with clients. And, worst of all, they couldn't switch seats on their return, so she had to sit next to him on a plane for fifteen hours. *No, that's fine, use the whole armrest, JUST LIKE YOU USED ME.*

The breakup itself didn't surprise me, but the fact that he had initiated it did—I thought for sure she would end it. During my only encounter with her boyfriend I'd deemed him unworthy. The reason? He ate mussels slowly. At a dinner for Evan's birthday, our whole group had to sit at the table for an extra thirty minutes while he finished eating. He would take a few minutes to prepare and eat every mussel and set down his fork between bites, as if he needed a rest after such physical exertion. Eleven of us sat watching him eat until well after the check had been paid.

His behavior was, at most, mildly annoying, but I found it maddening because of my attraction to Laura. There was a reason I'd messaged her online, after all. When a guy likes a girl, even one he knows he can't date, he will hate her boyfriends for totally irrational reasons. Thus, eating slowly made Laura's boyfriend completely unfit. *This beautiful woman deserves someone who eats at a normal speed. How does she put up with this MONSTER?*

I'd found Laura attractive from the first time I'd met her at college, which happened while visiting Maria in the basement of the film school where they were editing a project together. The two of them were huddled over the editing machine in a dark room and when they flipped on the lights upon my arrival, I was stunned by Laura's beauty. My mouth didn't drop open cartoon-wolf-style or anything, but I noticed her.

I was happily dating Maria, so Laura and I were never more than acquaintances in college, but her face was etched into my memory. When I became friends with Evan in LA and learned he'd dated Laura (aka Pretty Spanish Girl) in college, I was amazed. It was like he'd dated a celebrity. (I wasn't as memorable—the first time Laura and I met again, in LA, she confused me for my college roommate.)

All these years later, Laura remained beautiful enough to make it hard to focus on my poached eggs and applewood-smoked bacon. Her features were distinctly Mediterranean—olive skin, dark eyes—and she had a voluptuous body. And yes, great collarbones. I don't know if that's a Spanish trait or not, but hers were fantastic.

The more we talked about our failed relationships, the more I felt Laura and I were looking for the same thing, a stable partner who would show us the same loyalty and love we offered back.

A thought popped into my head: *I would like to date Laura.*

I quickly disregarded the impulse. Not only was she Evan's ex-girlfriend, she was also one of his current best friends, so, off-limits. I'd learned my lesson with Kurt's friend Amber, the pediatrician—no dating the friend of a friend (Kurt still couldn't bring me to certain events).

And so, though a woman I suspected might be perfect for me sat across the table, for the good of my friendship with Evan, I tweaked the thought. *I would like to date Laura* became *I would like to date someone LIKE Laura.* Because the world is teeming with beautiful Spanish women who have successful careers, a keen sense of humor, and a gorgeous smile. I'd probably run into one on the way out of the restaurant.

26

THE ACCIDENTAL
BORN-AGAIN VIRGIN

"I've been on only one date in the last six years."

I froze, a dim sum dumpling perched in my chopsticks. Cassidy took a sip of her Sapporo. Our second date had consisted of the usual getting-to-know-you chitchat, up to this revelation.

We'd met a few weeks earlier during the intermission of a show I was hosting. I'd sworn not to date another "groupie," but that rule came with the ever-present invisible parenthetical *(unless she's hot)*. Cassidy was a few years older than me, almost forty, but had the face and toned body of a younger woman, thanks no doubt to the usual Los Angeles cures for aging—yoga, juicing, and feasting on wolf placenta.

Our first date had gone well and the second was going just as smoothly until her revelation about being single-and-not-at-all-ready-to-mingle for the last six years. A few seconds after the announcement I was still holding the chopsticks in front of me, thinking of how to respond. A drop of soy sauce slid down the dumpling and fell to the table.

"I didn't plan it," she continued. "I had a rough breakup and took a breather from dating altogether. A little break turned into six years. I work from home and I'm kind of shy, so I haven't really met anyone. Until you."

I should have moved on to normal second-date questions, asked if she liked to travel or what her favorite movies were, but I couldn't deny my curiosity.

"So, does that mean you haven't had sex in six years?"

The hue her cheeks turned answered the question before she said, "I haven't."

"Wow," was all I could manage.

"I'm not a virgin or anything," she said. "I actually quite like sex."

"Well, that's good. Me too."

We both grinned as we realized this conversation was no longer a generic sex talk, but about the possibility of our coupling. I let the topic drop and finally ate the dumpling dangling in front of me.

At the end of the night, while we waited for her car at the valet station, I leaned in with the intent of a brief, introductory kiss. She had other ideas, wrapping her arms around me and pressing up close. I could feel the warmth of her body through her thin dress as I got the type of kiss one might expect from a woman who's waited six years to kiss someone. We made out for several minutes and might have gone on for hours if the valet hadn't pulled her car up. She skipped around to the driver's side and waved happily as she drove off.

"I think she likes you," the valet said as he took my ticket.

———

For our third date, I invited Cassidy over to my house for dinner. Normally, this would mean sex, but given Cassidy's history, I didn't know what would happen. It wasn't her first time, but it was her first time in a long time, so she might need more time before our first time. And if she *did* want to have sex, was I up for the pressure? I wouldn't be representing only myself, but sex in general, like the UN Ambassador of Intercourse. What if in the past six years she'd built sex up in her imagination to be an extraordinary phenomenon I couldn't match? I didn't want our session to end with her saying, "Well, I don't need that again for another half decade."

———

During dinner the sexual tension acted as an adhesive and kept our words stuck to our tongues. After the quiet meal we moved to the couch and started kissing. Only a few minutes in, she said, "I want to have sex."

"Are you sure?"

"It's been six years. I'm VERY sure."

I led her into the bedroom and everything was normal—she remembered how to do it and seemed to enjoy herself, though she didn't have an orgasm. Being a gentleman, I offered to help her get there using the nonintercourse methods.

"I don't let guys do that," she said, referring to oral sex. "It's okay that I didn't have an orgasm. I've actually never had an orgasm with someone else."

"Have you ever had an orgasm at all?"

"Yes, I have. I mean, when I'm on my own, when I . . ." She couldn't bring herself to say the word *masturbate*. "Can we stop talking about this?"

I nodded and we both lay back on our pillows. I felt bad for being so forward. Frank talk about sex is important, but given Cassidy's recent lack of experience, I'd probably been too forthright and explicit. It's one thing to ask questions, another for the post-coital talk to take on a patient-gynecologist dynamic. *No orgasms, eh? Let's get you up in the stirrups and have a look.*

After a few minutes of silence, she propped herself up on her elbow and faced me.

"No one's asked me about this stuff before," she said. "Thank you for caring and asking."

"You're welcome."

—————

Over eggs Benedict, I told the guys about my date with the Accidental Born-Again Virgin.

"So, it sounds like it was a good experience for both of you," Kurt said.

"Yeah, it went pretty well. I felt like I handled the situation with maturity and class. I was proud to welcome her back to the world of sexual activity."

The experience showed me how comfortable I'd become with sex during the last year. In the past, having sex was like observing a deer in nature—enjoy the beauty, but stay quiet so you don't scare it away. Now, not only could I have conversations about sex, but I could get others to open up about it too. It was gratifying that I'd helped Cassidy feel that her pleasure was important and worthy of discussion.

"Last night Evan came over. We watched TV and ate yogurt-covered pretzels," Kurt said. "It was Evan's first time. I was proud to welcome him into the world of yogurt pretzels."

"He did it with maturity and class. I felt so safe," Evan mocked.

They were taking the piss, as friends should. I'd had sex with a woman, not gone to Africa to feed the poor. I would take Sexual Philanthropist off my résumé when I got home.

———

Cassidy did not want another six years to pass before she had sex again. Our next date came quickly, arranged via a series of suggestive texts. That night, during dinner, she thanked me for not treating her as "damaged goods" just because she hadn't dated in a while. As we talked she was brimming with the early-relationship excitement. I couldn't match her enthusiasm. My mind was somewhere else. I was thinking about Laura.

She had been coming out with Evan more since she became single, and with every interaction my crush grew stronger. Though my mind remained resolute about not dating her, my body was staging a mutiny. Seeing Laura arrive at a party or hearing she'd be joining us for a drink made my heart jump. Pedestrian conversations about TV or traffic had my stomach flipping. I felt nervous every time I was around Lau. (I'd learned she usually went by Lau—pronounced like *loud* without the *d*—instead of Laura.)

I had tickets to a concert that week, and should have asked Cassidy to be my date, but I didn't want to take her. I wanted to go with Lau, so we could spend some time alone together, so I could see if my crush was real.

I couldn't just ask Lau to go with me, because that would be a date, so I devised a plan. I would ask Evan and Kurt first and, because they weren't huge music fans, they'd probably say no. I could then ask Lau as a "backup" option and it wouldn't be a date; I'd just be trying to get rid of a ticket at the last minute. My ploy worked and Lau agreed to join me.

It was a "secret" acoustic show and because cool things always have to be uncomfortable, we were seated on a dirty carpet in a converted garage. Normally, I would dread such a cramped setup, but I loved sitting shoulder to shoulder with Lau as we passed a tallboy beer back and forth. When our knees or elbows bumped together I could feel her touch on my skin for a few seconds, slowly fading like a blip on a radar screen.

After the show we lingered by our cars, trying to extend the night a little further. Being around Lau felt comfortable and exciting at the same time. I hadn't felt this electricity with Ella or Cassidy. It was a perfect first date. Except for the fact that it wasn't a date.

The night ended with a friendly hug and I went home alone, but I knew I no longer wanted to date someone *like* Lau. I wanted to date Lau herself. Not casually or just for sex. I wanted to date her for real, to be her boyfriend. I didn't know if the feelings were mutual, but I wanted to find out, which meant breaking it off with Cassidy.

Trying to let her down easy, I lied and told Cassidy I wasn't looking for anything serious. As I suspected, she was only interested in a relationship. We agreed to part ways, but a week later, I got an email from her. She'd changed her mind. Cassidy said she'd enjoyed our sexual chemistry and felt maybe it was time to change the way she dated. A casual, sexual relationship with me interested her and she went into some pretty exciting detail about what that could entail.

The email was tangible proof of my dating and sexual prowess, the exact sort of validation I'd wanted when I'd started my dating experiment. But, despite it being one of the most flattering emails I'd ever received, I didn't take Cassidy up on her offer. Though I wasn't dating Lau, I didn't want to sleep with anyone but her. And so I did something I couldn't have imagined doing a year and a half earlier—I turned down sex. And I did it for a woman who might not even like me.

Finding out if Lau was interested in me would be tricky. Evan would be understandably sensitive about two of his friends seeing each other. It could ruin our friendship. Bros' Brunch seemed like an institution, something that was eternal, like the IRS or Tom Cruise, but this could bring it to an end if not handled well.

27

CASUAL DATING:
WHAT'S THAT?

In the time since I'd taken Lau to the concert, Evan had made a few passive-aggressive comments, things like *Are there membership cards for the Best Friends Concert Club* or *When is Lau officially taking my place in Bros' Brunch?* One night while we were watching basketball at my house, Evan asked me about it directly. Or as directly as Evan could manage.

"I would hope that if, like, two of my friends were dating, they would let me know."

"I assume you're talking about Lau and me?"

"Well, I'm talking about any of my friends, but yeah, that includes you and Lau. Obviously, I don't own her or you, and you can do what you want, but I hope you won't keep anything from me."

His feelings were totally natural—he didn't want two close friends doing things behind his back. I told him I did have a crush on Lau, but nothing had happened and I didn't know if anything ever would. I promised to keep him in the loop as things progressed. He thanked me and relaxed a little, though I could tell this wouldn't be our last conversation on the matter. Ironically, Evan's concern about us liking each other led to a confirmation that we did. The next morning I had an email from Lau:

Evan told me you two talked. Maybe I shouldn't have told him I have a crush on you. For what it's worth, I am thankful it's made me snap out of my shit with my ex a bit and it reminds me that there are a lot of great people out there. Please don't be weird with me. We can be friends. I can keep my crush under control. You won't even notice. Friends?

I wrote her back, thanking her for being honest, and confirmed my crush on her. We agreed to stay friends, at least for now. But it's hard for people to act normal when they know they like each other. In my effort to make it seem like I didn't like her I stopped just short of acting like an elementary school boy who's been asked if he has a girlfriend. *NOOOO! I DON'T LIKE ANYONE. SHUT UP! GIRLS ARE GROSS!*

For example, one hot day, Evan and I went to Lau's condo complex to use the pool. Shortly after arriving I asked Evan to apply the sunscreen to my back.

"Uh, I'm sure Lau can do that for you," Evan said.

There is an unwritten dude rule about the order in which you request help with sunscreen. First, you ask a female. If one is unavailable, you squirt the lotion on a tree and rub your back against it. If both those fail, you may ask a male friend. In an attempt to act "normal" I was going too far in the other direction.

Lau and I spent two months swapping long emails in which we discussed everything except how we felt about each other. Two months of longing but fleeting eye contact across a table during group dinners. Two months of hugs that lingered a beat longer than they did with anyone else. The only thing that came close to a conversation about being romantic came one night at a bar when Lau said, unprompted, "I don't do casual."

"I don't have to do casual," I protested. "I can do serious dating."

"Mm-hmm," she said, with pursed lips and raised eyebrows. She'd heard all my dating stories from Evan and was rightfully skeptical.

In our two months as "friends" it became clear this was more than simple attraction or a short-lived crush. There was a chance of something special between us, which meant it was time to have another discussion with Evan. Not so I could ask "permission" (we're not medieval lords or frat brothers), but to make sure it wouldn't affect our friendship.

"So, how long has it been since you and Lau broke up?" I asked.

We were again watching basketball at my house.

"Nine years."

I hadn't known it had been THAT LONG. When Evan and Lau broke up, YouTube, Twitter, the iPhone, and Facebook didn't yet exist. Basically, they'd broken up before time began.

"Nine years is a pretty long time, right?" I said.

"I was never nervous about you dating Lau because she's my ex. I don't think of her that way anymore," Evan explained. "I was nervous because I've watched you date girl after girl and I didn't want you to add Lau to the list."

"So you just didn't want to see a good friend get hurt?"

"Well, mostly I was thinking about how awkward it would be for me if it didn't work out. But yeah, that too."

Evan was being self-effacing, but his effort to protect his friends and friendships was touching. I'd worried he would be a jealous ex, but it was clear now he was more like a protective big brother.

"I really like Lau," I said, "and I want to give it a serious go. Would you be okay with that?"

"As long as you can promise to never break up, yeah, I'm totally fine with it."

"I'll do my best."

"In all seriousness," Evan said, "I'm okay with it. I know I've been weird about this whole thing, but I do think you guys would be good together. And I think you're ready for a relationship again."

I'd wanted his blessing concerning Lau, but his statement about my being ready in general meant just as much.

———

A group of us were going camping on Memorial Day weekend. Lau and I agreed it would be best if we spent time alone together before going out into the woods to drink a lot of whiskey, but the only night that worked was Friday, the night before we were to leave. Which led to this text message from Lau:

> So, I think we need to make it a sleepover date. I would normally NEVER do that on a first date, but we're meeting at your house early on Saturday for camping, and I live far away, so it makes the most sense. But don't feel pressured to have sex.

After countless dates, I thought I'd gotten over being nervous, but I could barely eat that day. Knowing it was a sure thing—Lau was sleeping over, after all—didn't allay my anxiety, for this was no longer about succeeding or failing, getting laid or not. It was about finally testing a connection I desperately wanted to be real.

Lau's arrival wasn't romantic. Having survived ninety minutes of rush-hour traffic, she pushed by me for the bathroom, shedding two large bags full of camping gear as she went. I sat on the couch drying my sweaty palms on my pant legs. When she emerged, I stood up.

"Where are we going to dinner?" she asked.

I took a couple steps toward Lau and caught a whiff of her perfume, sweet and floral.

"Mexican sound good?"

Another step closer. Those big eyes, that wide smile.

"Love Mexican."

I was standing right in front of her now.

"Good. There's a great little place near here."

I pulled Lau toward me and kissed her.

CUT TO:

INT. LIVING ROOM—NIGHT

As Matteson and Lau kiss, we ZOOM IN on the microscopic space between their lips where we see:

A SPARK.

It's tiny, imperceptive to the naked eye, only visible on a nuclear level.

The camera PULLS BACK quickly, away from the couple, out the window, up into the sky, and finally off the planet.

We see our solar system, but something strange is happening: the Earth isn't orbiting the sun any longer. Instead the sun is orbiting Earth, as are the other planets. In the background the stars of the Milky Way obediently circle as well. Matteson and Laura are at the center of it all for a split second.

Snap back into motion, ZOOMING in at an incredible pace, through the solar system, down to Earth, and back inside the apartment just in time to see the kiss end.

The two pull apart, smile at each other, and then exit the apartment, off to do what one should always do after a galactic superevent—eat tacos.

END SCENE

(Or at least that's kind of what it felt like.)

———

After a whole book of telling you way (WAY) too much about my sex life, I won't tell you much about what happened with Lau that night. I want to keep those details to myself. I will say that despite her text message, she did pressure me into having sex (I forgave her) and it was better than any of the other sex I'd had.

The next morning we went camping with our friends and spent

the weekend hiking, swimming, cooking out, roasting marshmal-lows, and drinking around a fire. Lau and I shared a tent and cud-dled together under one sleeping bag. Both Evan and Kurt were there, but it wasn't awkward at all. Evan did leave a day early, but that had nothing to do with Lau and me; he just didn't want to poop outdoors.

After avoiding commitment for so long, that weekend I told Lau I wanted to be exclusive, making us a couple before the end of what was technically still our first date. And I didn't stop there—within two weeks I'd told her I loved her and this time there was no wondering if I meant it. I wasn't falling in love or maybe in love or trying to be in love—this was full-on, head-over-heels, all-the-way, no-doubt love. And she felt the same way.

My mental connection with Ella had seemed like an improve-ment over infatuation, but all head was just as flawed as all heart. You can't persuade yourself to love someone, no matter how much you agree on which TV shows are good. With Lau, I finally had both parts of the equation. My attraction to her got the infatuation chemicals in my brain pumping, but our long history ensured there was a foundation of friendship beneath those feelings.

And yes, she checked off everything on my precious List.

- **Shit together**—She was a vice president at her company.
- **Low-maintenance**—Going to a place with no toilets for three days on your first date is a good way to verify this.
- **Like AND love**—Had to like her before I loved her.
- **Had long-term important friendships/relationships**—Duh, Evan. She was almost TOO good at this one.

- **Truly respect my partner**—She was one of the most impressive and smart people I knew.

After months of calculating every move and intellectualizing my emotions, everything with Lau was easy and natural. There was no Plotting Points, no worrying about what anything meant, no nervousness about having The Talk, no playing it cool. I told Lau exactly how much I liked her and saw her as often as I could. I'd fallen in love before, but joining my life with someone else had never been this easy. One month into our relationship, a small issue did pop up, though—Lau was being kicked out of the country.

A lawyer for Lau's company had filed some Green Card sponsorship paperwork improperly and she'd been denied because of the technicality. Though she'd lived in the States for more than fifteen years and the clerical error was explainable, the government didn't care. Lau reapplied under a different method, but there was a catch—she couldn't stay in the country while her secondary application was under consideration. She had ninety days to leave.

I'd gotten over my heartbreak, navigated the world of casual dating, saved myself from being the Sleazy Guy, started dating a friend's ex-girlfriend with ambassador-level diplomacy, and fallen in love with a wonderful woman. I'd fucking pulled this thing off, but the universe was like, *Come on, silly mortal, give me a break with these life plans of yours. You know who else had plans? The dinosaurs.*

Though we'd only dated a short time, Lau and I didn't consider breaking up. Instead, I would make an extended visit to Spain while Lau waited for her paperwork to come through. I'd been looking for a good excuse to leave my job and this was it—I'd live in Barcelona for a few months, write, and get to know her family. Hopefully, during my time there she'd get her Green Card and we'd return together.

I was excited about this plan—who wouldn't want to live in Barcelona for three months?—but anxious. The Green Card process could take a few months or it could take years, and when dealing with the federal government it's usually smart to bet on the "Over." Another denial was possible too. Lau's lawyer was confident in her case, but there was no guarantee.

We enjoyed the summer, but Lau's imminent departure loomed. Luckily, we had a big event coming up to distract us—we were going to Burning Man together a few weeks before she had to leave.

———

Burning Man can be difficult for some couples because of the intense partying and sexuality, but it was a wonderful week for us. One moment in particular showed me just how hard I'd fallen for Lau. We were back at our yurt after a night of exploring the Playa and I was feeling lucky to be sharing the experience with someone I loved.

"I'm so glad you're here with me," I said.

"Me too," she said.

"I love . . . WAAAAHHHH."

I couldn't finish my thought because I began sobbing. Not a few tears, not a light cry, but all-out WAILING. My body shook and snot dripped down my face and my abdominal muscles began to hurt I was heaving so hard. I am not normally a crier—I've emerged from every Pixar movie with dry cheeks—but I could not stop.

"What's wrong?" Lau asked.

I couldn't respond, couldn't do anything but cry. Lau pulled me close and comforted me until I finally stopped ten minutes later.

"Sorry about that," I said, wiping my eyes. "I don't know what happened, I just wanted to tell you that I really love— WAAAAAAHHHH . . ."

And I was crying again, just as hard as the first time. I'd told Lau I loved her hundreds of times before, but now I couldn't get past the *o* in the L-word without a complete breakdown. I was feeling in totality what I was trying to say and it was short-circuiting my emotional system. (This may or may not have happened on Acid Monday.) Luckily, Lau was touched, rather than mortified.

On the last day of the week, as I watched the fire burn up the Temple, a deep sadness hit me. The flames signaled not only the end of Burning Man, but also Lau's departure. As I stared at the fire an idea popped into my head: *I should marry Laura.*

Though I'd never been outright antimarriage, I was cynical about the institution, thanks to my parents' divorce. In order to avoid my parents' fate, I'd decided at a young age I wouldn't get married until after thirty (check) and only after many years of dating and cohabitation with my intended wife. Before I got married, I wanted to have done a lot of research and seen all my options. Basically, I wanted to treat marriage like buying a printer on Amazon.

But, only three months into my relationship, the idea of marrying Lau didn't scare me or strike me as a dumb idea. It wasn't just that I didn't want her to leave in a few weeks; I didn't want her to ever leave. I wanted Lau to be my wife. I realized I'd put off marriage not because I didn't believe in it, but because I so badly wanted to get it right. At the core of every cynic is a true believer.

I contemplated dropping to my knee right there and asking, but I didn't, because while getting married seemed like a good idea, A LOT of things seem like a good idea at Burning Man. A day earlier I'd thought a food truck for dogs called Puppy Ciao was a million-dollar idea. A year earlier I'd practically proposed to a man despite not being homosexual. Yes, marriage seemed like a good idea, but as a general rule, one shouldn't make a major life decision in the same week they've dropped acid twice.

———

I should marry Laura.

The thought was still echoing in my head the next day as we drove back to Los Angeles.

I should marry Laura.

It stayed with me into the next week, persisting long after I'd fully rested and rehydrated, beyond when any drugs could have possibly remained in my system.

I should marry Laura.

After two weeks I gave in to the thought. I was going to ask her to be my wife.

She was leaving in six days, so there was no time for an elaborate proposal or even a ring. The night I decided, Lau came over to my apartment for dinner. I'd wanted to bring up marriage in some sort of romantic way, but halfway through cooking the meal I couldn't bear to wait any longer, so I took the pot of rice I was stirring off the burner, dried my hands on a towel, and said, "What if we got married?"

Lau didn't scream *Oh my God yes*, leap to her feet, or start crying. She remained in her seat, her reaction tempered.

"I mean, we've talked about that in the past a little bit," she said, "but we didn't want my immigration situation to drive the decision. Why are you thinking differently now?"

"If your Green Card gets denied in six months, we'd get married then. Why not do it now and save us both the money and the heartache of being apart?"

Lau kept her arms crossed.

"I don't want you to marry me as a favor or because it's convenient. I've had boyfriends suggest it in the past and I've never wanted to do it that way."

I hadn't expected to have to convince Lau she should marry me and stay in the country.

"It's true that if it weren't for the outside factors, I probably wouldn't be proposing this soon. But that doesn't mean it's a 'favor.' Us getting married feels like a matter of when, not if. I've spent the last two weeks trying to convince myself that it's idiotic to marry someone I've only been with four months, but I can't, because it feels right. I know it's a little crazy, but I don't care. I've found the woman I'm supposed to marry. I have no doubts about you or us or getting married."

Lau finally let the veneer fall. Her mouth widened into a smile as she sprang from her chair and grabbed me in an embrace.

"I don't have any doubts, either," she said. "I love you so much."

"So are we doing it, then? We're getting married?"

"Yes!"

We hugged and cried and called our (somewhat surprised) family. After things had settled down a little bit, I apologized for the informal proposal. Not only was it missing the traditional accompaniments—flowers, a ring, a bended knee—but I'd been in the middle of cooking. There's a reason Uncle Ben's Wild Rice has never made an appearance in a fairy tale.

"I'm sorry this wasn't more romantic," I said.

"It was perfect," she responded. "Proposing to me so soon has to be a little scary, but you did it anyway because you love me and you believe in us. There's nothing more romantic than that."

In this book, I've spent a lot of time explaining how things don't happen like they do in the movies, but you know what? Sometimes they do.

28

THE OPPOSITE OF A
VERY LONG ENGAGEMENT

In order to apply for Lau's Green Card, we needed to get married right away, which meant a courthouse wedding, just like the one my stepbrother had had two years before. I guess I was ready to admit that love just might be real.

The courthouse wedding process in Los Angeles is very easy—a few simple forms, no blood test, dates available within a week. And it only costs $149.50. This was like an infomercial product too good to be true. *For this low, low price you get fifteen minutes in a courthouse chapel, a certified judge, and we'll throw in not one, but TWO, official copies of the marriage certificate. Operators are standing by to make your love eternal.*

Lau and I had envisioned a tiny ceremony to make it legal, followed by the "real" wedding a year or so later, but everyone wanted to be there for the first go-round. Most of our family was going to make it, mine flying in from Colorado and Lau's from Spain. So many friends wanted to attend, we surpassed the twenty-person capacity of the small chapel, necessitating an informal "reception" of sorts. We didn't rent out a banquet hall or event space, or even make

a reservation. Instead, we told everyone to meet us at a Mexican restaurant that had a nice patio and a hell of a deal on Happy Hour
guacamole. Having seen friends lose a year of their lives and most
of their bank accounts to wedding planning, I highly recommend
the "We need to make this legal as quickly as possible" approach to
marriage.

At first, our wedding didn't seem much different from a visit to
the DMV, complete with lines full of people sporting bureaucracy-
inspired blank stares. While we were there to sanctify our love,
everyone else was waiting to file construction permits or pay park-
ing fines. We checked in with an impatient employee who ended
our interaction with the official slogan of government offices, "Go
stand over there and we'll call your name."

The wedding party before us emptied from the chapel and someone called, "Perry party? Are you ready?" as if our table had been
wiped down at Red Lobster. I took Lau's hand and we entered the
chapel, though it was a "chapel" in name only. The room had a hung
tile ceiling, fluorescent lights, and a carpet that had probably out-
lasted many of the marriages performed on it. A small wooden arch
strewn with fake purple flowers served as the only decoration, and as
we entered, prerecorded organ music started up. So, all very similar
to a royal wedding.

A tiny woman, no more than five feet tall, waited at the front of
the room in a black judge's cloak. She had to be at least eighty years
old and her wrinkles, produced by decades in the California sun,
were dark and numerous.

"I'm going to be marrying you today," she said, sounding like a grandma welcoming her grandkids to Christmas. "Isn't that wonderful?"

Her smile melted away all the government coldness we'd experienced up to this point. It was wonderful!

I glanced back at the assembled party. It was standing-room only, packed with all the people I loved most in my life. Our parents stood next to each other in the front. Grant darted around the room acting as our official photographer and Kurt stood in the back. One important person was missing, though: Evan was running late. And this was more than a sentimental problem. He was supposed to sign the wedding certificate as our official witness. We'd asked him to do the honor because of the integral part he'd played in the formation of our relationship. Proud to make the rare jump from cock-block to wedding witness, he had accepted readily, but now someone else would have to sign. It was a shame, but the $149.50 only got us fifteen minutes. We couldn't wait for him.

"A ring has no beginning and no end," the judge began. "It is endless, just like your love for one another. It is a symbol of your commitment to your relationship, a commitment that will last FOREVER."

On the final word, *forever*, the judge locked eyes with me, implying via stare that, despite the modest stature of the ceremony, I needed to take my vows seriously, OR ELSE. In addition to legally wedding us, the old lady may also have been casting a Gypsy curse.

As the judge gazed into my soul, I felt the full weight of what I was doing. Lau and I had been together for only a few months, engaged for just two weeks, but that didn't make this ceremony, this marriage, any less real. We were getting married today and there was no way to know if our marriage would be a beautiful story or an epic disaster, whether it would last decades or days. But the uncertainty didn't scare me.

In my life I'd made so many choices based on fear—fear of being alone, failing, being uncool, not getting laid, being unworthy, losing control. But this choice was not based in fear. I wasn't marrying Lau because it felt like I "should" or because she'd be mad if I didn't or because I feared being alone. I was marrying Lau because I wanted to make her my wife, because I felt ready for and worthy of both her and the institution. I didn't know how our marriage would end, because no marriage has a guarantee, but I knew how it would begin: without fear or trepidation. And that's the best anyone can hope for.

The judge got to the end of her speech and we both said "I do." It'd been eleven years since I'd met Lau, a year and a half since we'd messaged online, four months since we'd started dating, two weeks since I'd proposed, and twelve minutes since we'd entered the chapel/conference room, and, with those two words, we were now husband and wife. It was a whirlwind romance twelve years in the making.

The last step was to sign the marriage certificate.

"Who's going to be the witness?" the judge asked.

We started to wave over our friend Olivier, Evan's backup, but before he could stand, there was a shout from the back.

"I'm the witness. The witness is here!"

Evan strode to the front.

"Wouldn't have missed it," he said, like an action hero arriving to save the day just in the nick of time. Four signatures and two minutes later Lau and I were married and the room erupted into applause.

EPILOGUE

Well, I really lucked into the happy ending I'd been trying so hard to convince myself was nonexistent. I mean, we were one rush-to-the-courthouse-on-the-back-of-a-moped away from this being exactly like the end of a romantic comedy. But, of course, weddings aren't an end, but a beginning.

———

A few months after our wedding, we had our Green Card interview. Seeing as our marriage was real, the interview was a formality, but it was still terrifying to know that our fate lay in the hands of a government employee.

I'd expected someone in a suit or a uniform, but our case agent wore a tank top and a government-issued Windbreaker. Because Lau had lived in the country more than fifteen years, her case file was frighteningly thick, rising three inches off of the desk. We'd come armed with dozens of pictures of our time together, from our camping trip to our wedding, along with a printed screenshot of our Facebook page showing our status as "Married." If there was any doubt, that would clinch it—people might move in together to pull off a fake marriage, but who would lie on Facebook?

The questions started simple—how'd we met, where'd we gone on our first date, what was our wedding like—but soon things got intimate. The agent leaned forward in her chair and looked at me.

"So how did you know Laura was the one?"

This didn't seem like a question a government official would ask, but rather, something Oprah would pose to a guest. If only I'd had this book completed then—*Read this and you'll see the emotional and spiritual journey that led me to falling in love with Lau. It's kind of like* Eat, Pray, Love, *but by a dude. Please give it a good review on Amazon if you like it!*

I tried to summarize my feelings for Lau, but it's hard to do that without sounding like a dumb athlete talking about winning the Super Bowl. You end up saying things like "amazing" and "hard to describe" and "just knew." I could tell this boilerplate material didn't impress the agent, so I dug deeper.

"I think, besides the general feelings of love, I knew Lau was the one because we were friends first."

Lau squeezed my hand when I said this. Not in a *that's-so-sweet* kind of way, but in a *what-the-fuck-are-you-doing* kind of way. When trying to assure an immigration agent you didn't fake a marriage as a favor to a friend, it may not be best to mention how you started as friends. But I was going somewhere with this, so I continued.

"In the past I've had relationships where I thought it was love, but with time it faded and I realized it had just been attraction and infatuation, rather than a true connection. But I knew Lau well before we dated. She was a friend I valued. So when the romantic feelings came, it was a wonderful combination of romantic love and friendship, which is what I think truly makes someone a soul mate."

The agent gazed at me as she formulated her response. Shit— was she not buying this? Had I screwed up so badly that I'd convinced her my real marriage was a fake marriage?

Finally she spoke.

"I hear that. You've got to have a solid base, because the other stuff fades. Mmm-hmmm."

She nodded emphatically, making it clear she was speaking from experience. We were no longer government official and investigation subject, but rather two best girlfriends gabbing at the hair salon. Ten minutes later Lau was officially granted her Green Card.

———

As I write this, Lau and I have been happily married for over two years. Pretty quickly we abandoned the idea of throwing another wedding; it's hard to dedicate the time and money required when you're already married. Instead, for our first act as responsible, married adults, we quit our jobs and took a two-month honeymoon to Europe and Asia.

I've claimed to learn a lot of things in this book, but if I can impart just one thing, it is this: marry someone from Barcelona. We spent two weeks in Lau's hometown on our trip and it was so *choice.* For the rest of my life, instead of going to, say, Albuquerque, to visit the in-laws, I get to go there. I will constantly be saying things like *We just got back from such a lovely holiday in Europe. Holiday is what we call vacation in Europe. You simply must join us next time, old sport.* Will my friends find this annoying? Sure. But I don't care, because I'll have better, tanner friends in Barcelona.

We still see Kurt and Evan almost every week for drinks, dinner, or brunch (Bros' Brunch gained a gal). Kurt remains happily single, open to meeting someone, but not worried about it, and Evan is still Joanna-free. As he braves the waters of online dating I act as his consigliere, even when he hasn't asked for the advice. (Approximately 80% of my advice is unsolicited.)

Grant is up the road in San Francisco, having settled with a wonderful woman after going on a journey of his own. He spent a year traveling the world, doing everything from drinking ayahuasca in South America to summiting peaks in Nepal. And he is now a Drug Spirit Guide to the world as one of the hosts of a podcast about psychedelics.

Brian is in Toronto, so we're doing the long-distance thing. It's hard, but he's worth it. (Lau is amazingly accepting of our relationship.)

ACKNOWLEDGMENTS

I'd like to thank the following people without whom this book would not have been possible:

My wife, Laura, for being my happy ending.

My mom, Krista, for always being my protector and supporter.

My dad, Jim, for inspiring me to be a writer by filling my childhood with stories and a love of books.

Katelin, for doing her sisterly duty of keeping me grounded with reminders that I'm not *that great.*

Sarah, Chris, and Stephen for the love and support.

Becky Sweren, my agent at Kuhn Projects, for believing enough in my writing to take on the gargantuan task of selling a book by a first-time writer. And, more importantly, for doing her best to make sure I didn't come across like a douchebag.

My editor, John Glynn, for the sound advice that made this book better at every turn and for understanding and believing in me and the material.

Everyone at Kuhn Projects, for working so hard to ensure the success of this book.

The whole team at Scribner, for helping me put together a final product of which I'm immensely proud. It's a true thrill to be under the banner.

Paul Shirley, for being a wonderful coffee shop writing buddy. I'm lucky to have him as a reader and friend.

To Brad, Carnie, Charles, Craig, Cuyler, Galen, Jay, Jesse, and many other close friends, who heard me tell the original version of these stories countless times.

Everyone in DeMentha, for the inspiration and an immeasurable amount of fun.

Ingo, for lowering himself to read this American love dribble and not completely crushing me with his feedback.

Jason Richman, for being an early believer in this project and a great agent.

Daniel Jones, the editor of the *New York Times* "Modern Love" column, for selecting my essay. Being published in "Modern Love" was the first step toward this book existing.

The Moth organization, and Gary Buchler, Kerry Armstrong, and Jenifer Hixson in particular. Many of the chapters in this book started as stories I told on the Moth stage.

Finally, thank you to all the women in this book. I hope you don't hate me.